Copyright

First printing 2017 ISBN 978-1-387-03713-1

Acknowledgements

First and foremost, I would like to thank Nathan Baker for offering the course that would inspire all of my research into this subject at the University of Oregon in 2008. I would also like to thank him for encouraging me to also teach a course on video game music. I would like to thank Dr. Jack Boss and Dr. Joelle Welling for allowing me to teach video game music at the University of Oregon and the University of Calgary, respectively. This text would not have been possible without the support of all of these people.

I would also like to thank my partner, Martin Ritter, for helping me make it through the completion of this text by offering emotional support and editing.

Foreword

This text is intended to serve as an introduction to the study of video game music. It was initially conceived as a companion to an introductory video game music course that takes a multi-faceted survey approach to the material. Therefore, this text can be used in accompaniment with an academic setting. It can also be useful for anyone that is generally interested in learning about video game music, but does not have a very solid musical or technical foundation. As it was intended to accompany a course in which non-music majors could freely enrol, the text is accessible to nearly everyone, and covers the topic of video game music very generally.

Chapter 1: Introduction and Methodology Overview

This chapter describes the approach this text takes, including the topics surveyed and methodology used. By the end of the chapter, you should understand:

1) What aspects of video game music are going to be studied in this text,
2) How we will go about studying these,
3) Some of the reasons behind why video game music is such a valuable field of study.

1.1 Objectives

This text introduces the study of video game music from a variety of perspectives, taking a survey approach. It is not designed to instruct the reader on how to compose for video games, nor how to break into the video game industry. However, it could be extremely useful to composers interested in writing for video games as it provides a comprehensive history of video game music, and discusses at length many of the techniques composers use to achieve certain effects. The text is broken into three primary sections, which represent different approaches with which to study video game music:

1) The history of video game music,
2) Musical and theoretical concepts, and
3) Sociocultural impact of video game music.

All of these approaches are written to be accessible to a diverse body of learners from many disciplines, and readers are encouraged to seek out the cited references to further increase their depth of understanding.

1.2 Methodology

As mentioned above, this text takes a survey approach. It introduces the reader to the study of video game music as an academic subject. We approach the study of video game music in much of the same way that western classical music is traditionally studied. Therefore, the methodology may seem very similar in this text to the study of music history. However, the history of video game music only compromises one of the sections of the text. This text takes a more comprehensive and critical approach, including theoretical concepts and more. The methodology of each section is described in more detail below:

1.2.1 History of Video Game Music
This section details the history of video game music, from the very beginnings of arcade games through the modern period. By the end of section one, you should be able to:

1) Identify several composers and games,
2) Identify qualities of music for specific console generations,
3) Understand the influence of technology on game sound, and
4) Gain knowledge about the reception of video game music and its impact in the community.

Like western music history studies, this section focuses a lot on the composers and their specific contributions to the development of game music and sound. This section traces the history of video game music and how the utility of the sound/music has impacted the musical styles. For example, in the early days of arcade games, music was used as a means to draw customers. Today, sound and music in games is designed to be immersive as possible because that is what current consumers demand and how the technology is trending. Therefore, our historical approach will not only focus on the sound of the music and who composed it, but on the context under which it was composed. We will also study the impact of technology development on video game music. Storage space and memory, for example, contribute to the amount of information an individual game can contain and a system can access. Therefore, music programmers, who sought to use small amounts of data to create unending pieces of music, often composed (programmed) early music. Later on, more efficient machines and larger storage mediums allowed for the use of streaming audio that loops, or continues endlessly through some other means.

1.2.2 Musical and Theoretical Concepts
By the end of this section, you should understand:

1) Interactive media-specific terminology and concepts,
2) Form and function of video game music,
3) Storytelling and characterization devices, and

4) Use of sound effects and immersive sound environments.

This section examines some of the musical and theoretical concepts that are specific to video game music, or more generally, music for interactive media. Terminology specific to all media (including film and television) is discussed as well as terminology specific to interactive media and games. This chapter also covers the use of sound and musical devices for storytelling, mood capture, and environmental design, and includes some basic music theory of video game music. This text does not cover Roman numeral or harmonic analysis. This topic will be covered later in a small supplement to this text that will be accessible primarily to those who have already studied basic music theory. In this text we will also examine how theoretical concepts have evolved between console generations as the needs of the users have changed. The evolution of the role of sound effects is also discussed, since sound effects are becoming increasingly more important in video games.

1.3 Why Study Video Game Music, Anyways?

Now that you have been introduced to the concepts we are going to cover throughout this book, you may be wondering why it is so important to study video game music. Why would one want to study a popular and generally commercial genre of music in a scholarly setting? The study of western classical music, and more recently, serious music of all cultures, has dominated the field of musicology for a considerable amount of time, with nearly all academic output focused on this genre and relatively small timespan. Even musical eras such as the Medieval and early Renaissance and late 20th century to 21st century have been neglected in traditional academic literature, with a large emphasis placed on scholarship of the baroque through the early modern periods. In fact, it is only very recently that early music studies and contemporary musical studies (21st century and current) have become commonplace in the musicological community. It is important as a scholar of music to engage with all music and not view the entire music history with a very small lens, and lens that devalues commercial music. Recently, video game music has begun to see a small impact in the academic community, with several recent dissertations focusing on video game music,[1] courses developed and run on video game music,[2] and other texts being published

---

[1] See Medina-Gray, Elizabeth, "Modular Structure and Function in Early 21st Century Video Game Music," 2014, and Sextro, Justin Daniel, "Press start: narrative integration in 16-bit video game music," 2015.

[2] MUS 399: Sp St Video Game Music, University of Oregon, and MUSI 402 Topics

on the general subject. (Note: video game music as a commercial study has been around for a long time, but programs and courses that instruct in the subject tend to focus on the practical aspects of video game music, such as getting into the industry, and other technical or commercial focuses). Video game music is one of the most popular music genres of the current period. Although contemporary classical music can struggle to fill concert halls, for example, video game music concerts are very well attended, and generally by a younger demographic that is not commonly seen in classical concerts. There are entire music groups and acts that dedicate their careers to performing re-workings and remixes of video game music, such as The Black Mages and the Minibosses. Video games themselves are ubiquitous, and this is especially so with the popularity of mobile devices that contain ever-increasing storage and processing capacity. Entire video games can be stored in a singular iPhone application, making them more accessible than ever - there is no longer a need to purchase an extra expensive device to play full-length video games. Therefore, with such an impact and such a large audience, video game music might be one of the most listened to genres of music of our time. And yet the academic and reflective study of the genre is still emerging - while video game music studies courses are taught as supplemental or special studies courses, they have yet to exist within the common or core conservatory curriculum, even as suggested electives. And this is unfortunate, since the study of such can be important to aspiring composers of video game music (and other music) who hope to have a deeper understanding of musical context and meaning. The interactive nature of video game music also makes the study of it useful to many in fields including multimedia, sound design, and interaction design.

in Popular Music: Video Game Music, University of Calgary, instructed by Alyssa Aska

Chapter 2: Technology and Sound Basics

This chapter will present a brief *overview* of some of the music technology concepts that are pertinent to video game music. You will learn about the types of sound generation used in video games and some of the basic technological constructs and terminology. This will provide you with a framework and context with which to understand how and why video game music functions as it does - after all, the style and function of video game music is a result of available technology. In much the same way that the symphony sound is dependent on the development of the classical orchestra and the instruments within, so it is the case with video game music and technological forces. Composers have to work within the technological limitations of the console and create something effective with these means.

2.1 Characteristics of Sound

Before we jump directly into a discussion regarding sound production, it is important to understand the five basic characteristics of a sound. Understanding these will be important as we discuss the qualities of game music by different composers and for different consoles. These sound characteristics are also what you will use as a focal point if, for example, you wish to analyze a piece of video game music. Each characteristic has an *objective* and a *subjective* quality. The characteristics are described in the subsequent table.

Impetus	Objective	Subjective	Subjective Result
Wave speed	Frequency	Pitch	Perceived note
Wave height	Amplitude	Volume	Perceived loudness
Wave makeup	Spectrum	Timbre	Perceived "colour"
Length of wave	Duration	Rhythm	Perceived timing
Sounding body	Location	Panning	Perceived place
Extrasonic			
Mechanical causality	Embodiment	Agential displacement	Perceived connection between sound and sound source

All of these characteristics are directly related to the properties of a sound wave. You may be already familiar with the idea that sound propagates through space in waves, but in case you are not, a brief description of how this works follows. Sound is created when a **sound source** or **agent** enacts a motion on an object that creates a period displacement of air molecules, resulting in **sound waves.** The properties of this displacement (i.e., the properties of the wave itself) are what contribute to how we hear sound. An example of this would be the plucking of a guitar string. An **agent** plucks a guitar string, which vibrates. The vibrations cause periodic displacements of air molecules, and the result is a sound wave, which we perceive as a specific pitch (the plucked note) dependent on the frequency (speed) of the wave. This frequency is measured in Hertz (Hz), or complete wave cycles per second. A sound wave that contains 40 full wave cycles each second has a frequency of 40 Hz for example. The amplitude represents the measurement of the air pressure displacement, which we perceive as volume; large amounts of displacement will result in a perceptually louder sound. The other property of sound waves that doesn't have a subjective correspondent is phase, and this refers a specified point in the wave cycle. It is not necessary to have a complete understanding of the precise physics behind this to access all of the information in this book, but it is helpful to have a context with which to frame the sound and technological aspects discussed. Below the five properties of sound, I have added a sixth property, related to the mechanical causality and perceived relationship between sound and sound source. This property is also useful to the study of video game music, especially when discussing sounds that the character makes or sounds within the environment. If these topics interest you and do wish to have a fuller understanding, I encourage you to seek out Peter Manning's *Electronic and Computer Music 4th edition.*

2.2 Sound Synthesis

It is important to understand the ways in which sound is generated on video game systems, especially as we discuss console-specific music, and its' sound characteristics. Sound **synthesis** refers to the creation of sound from scratch. This is in contrast to, for example, recording a sound and playing it back. Early video game composers all used sound synthesis as their primary sound generation method since it was more technologically feasible than recording and playing back large amounts of pre-recorded sound. Several types of synthesis are discussed below, all of which have been implemented in video game music.

Additive synthesis involves the combination of various generated waveforms at different phases, amplitudes, and frequencies, to create complex waveforms (complex sounds). When you hear a sound, the frequency you perceive as pitch is called the **fundamental**. In a sound created using additive synthesis, this is generally the lowest frequency present in the waveform. Frequencies above the fundamental that are present in the waveform are called **partials**. Usually frequencies that are whole number multiples of the fundamental are added to the fundamental, although this is not always the case (whole number multiples are **harmonic**, frequencies that are not whole number multiples are called **inharmonic**). Different combinations will produce a different waveform makeup, which results in a different spectrum or timbre. A computer chip uses voltages to control these generated waveforms (sometimes referred to as oscillators), and the desired frequencies, amplitudes, and phases can all be set by the sound programmer. In the case of video game music, additive synthesis is primarily used to create very specific types of waveforms. I will provide a basic description of some of these:

Pulse waves: These contain odd numbered harmonics only. If the fundamental is 100 Hz, the first couple of partials will be 300 Hz (fundamental x 3), 500 Hz (fundamental x 5) and 700 Hz (fundamental x 7). The harmonics of these partials are present in the ratio 1/harmonic number. All of these harmonics are in phase.

Triangle waves: These also contain odd-numbered harmonics only. However, the amplitude of each harmonic is scaled to 1/harmonic number squared (the amplitude of the second partial, which is the third harmonic, would therefore be 1/9th of the amplitude of the fundamental). Additionally, every other harmonic is 180 degrees out of phase.

Noise: Most early consoles contained a channel that could generate noise. There are a few different kinds of noise, but in general, noise contains a wide band of frequencies at equal amplitudes. White noise consists of all frequencies at equal amplitudes. Pink noise consists of all frequencies, but the amplitudes differ at each octave. Noise is usually not created using additive synthesis; there are special noise generators to do so.

Subtractive synthesis involves the use of devices called filters to remove or reduce (attenuate) portions of the sound. Subtractive synthesis can be used on generated noise (which contains all frequencies), or on waveforms generated by additive synthesis. There are several types of filters, all of which have a different effect. The most common types of filters are high pass, low pass, band pass, and notch.

High pass filters: These types of filters allow frequencies *above* a specified frequency to pass unaltered. All lower frequencies are attenuated (reduced in volume).

Low pass filters: These types of filters allow frequencies *below* a specified frequency to pass unaltered. All higher frequencies are attenuated.

Band pass filters: A user must supply two frequencies to these types of filter - all of the frequencies on the outside of this specified band of frequencies are attenuated.

Notch filters: Like band pass filters, a user also specifies two frequencies to these filters. However, the frequencies within the band are attenuated, and the outside frequencies are allowed to pass.

These represent the most widely implemented types of filters, but this list is not exhaustive. More complex filters are continually being designed and used in music software and hardware.

Frequency Modulation (FM) Synthesis was developed by John Chowning in 1973 and gained widespread use when it was implemented into the chip of many Yamaha synthesizers in the early 1980s.[3] FM synthesis has the benefit of using only two oscillators to create very rich and complex timbres. The concept underlying FM synthesis is derived from a stylistic technique usually used by musicians called vibrato. In instrumental and vocal technique, vibrato is stylistic application of periodic fluctuations of tone (an example of this is in opera - held notes contain a wavering sound - this is vibrato). When synthesizing sound, vibrato is created when a single oscillator is modified by using a second oscillator as a continuous control to change the first oscillator. Very low frequency oscillators (those that are so low they are inaudible, about 6 Hz) are used to change the pitch of the first oscillator, but since these oscillators are below the hearing range, the result is perceived as very small but periodic changes in pitch, rather than a timbral change. We refer to the first oscillator in FM synthesis as the **carrier,** and the second the **modifier.** When the frequency of the modifier is increased to the audible range (20 Hz and above), it begins to alter the timbre, rather than the pitch, of the carrier wave. In this way, FM synthesis allows for very complex and rich timbres with very limited material (only two simple sound waves); this is achieved because other waves, called sidebands, are generated above and below the carrier wave. FM Synthesis is theoretically complicated, and it is not necessary to have a complete understanding of how it works to read this text. If you wish to learn more about FM synthesis, both Barry Truax[4] and John Chowning[5] have extensive literature on the topic.

---

[3] see US. Patent 4,018,121, April 19, 1977
[4] Truax, Barry. "Tutorial for Frequency Modulation Synthesis," http://www.sfu.ca/~truax/fmtut.html.
[5] Chowning, John M. "The synthesis of complex audio spectra by means of frequency modulation." Journal of the Audio Engineering Society 21.7 (1973): 526-534.

All of the types of synthesis described above were made possible by computer chips called **Programmable Sound Generators** that allowed composers (or sound programmers) to write machine language to instruct the oscillators how to behave. These are essentially the synthesizers, also called sound cards, which produce the game's sound; these PSGs can be located in the console, arcade cabinet, or computer base.

2.3 Streaming Audio and Digital Sampling

The use of streaming audio in video games became possible as consoles grew more efficient at processing and as the game storage mediums became able to hold more data. Unlike synthesis, streaming audio allows a piece of music to be pre-composed and then stored on the disc for later playback (and looping) during gameplay. This type of technology became widespread when cartridge type consoles were replaced with consoles that used optical laser disc (CDs and DVDs). Audio information is stored digitally on these devices, so in order to understand how streaming audio works, I will provide a basic introduction to digital audio. Audio information is transmitted into a digital format via a process called **digital sampling,** which converts an analog representation of sound to a digital representation of sound by taking measurements of instantaneous amplitudes of the sampled sound at equally spaced time intervals. What this means is that when a sampled sound is played, digital snapshots are taken at a speed known as a **sampling rate.** The sampling rate for CD quality sound is 44,100 - meaning that 44,100 snapshots of the incoming sound are taken every second. Sampling rate therefore will have a high impact on the quality of the digital sound, as the more samples that are taken, the more precise the replica of the sound becomes. The second contributing factor to sound quality in digital audio is **bit depth.** The term "bit" may already be familiar as it is a common computer storage term, short for binary digit. The higher the bit depth, the more information that can be encoded per sample - this allows for finer resolution in waveform amplitude.

Therefore, regarding quality:
1) Higher sampling rate means more snapshots are taken = higher quality
2) Higher bit depth means more potential values for amplitude in waveforms = higher quality.

However, we have to consider the size of the storage medium, and the higher the bit depth and sampling rate, the higher amount of storage the sound files take up. The most common sampling rate used today is 44.1 kHz and 48 kHz; the most common bit depth used is 16- or 24-bit.

2.4 Summary

You have been given a very basic overview of the basic technology used in game sound. This chapter does not go into great detail regarding the physics of sound, and does not survey concepts such as software used to program games or specific environments and engines used in game sound design. These subjects are beyond the scope of this book, which aims to provide an introduction to video game music for scholars of all levels, including non-musicians. With this basic introduction behind you, you should have enough understanding to comprehend the material throughout the book.

SECTION I: HISTORICAL SURVEY OF VIDEO GAME MUSIC

Chapter 3: Early History, From the Arcade to the Living Room

This chapter surveys the beginnings of video game music, from the arcade generation through the 8-bit systems (such as NES) and the 16-bit systems (SNES and others). This chapter is by no means an exhaustive history of early video game music, but does introduce the reader to some of the most prominent composers, games, and technologies. By the end of this chapter, the reader should be able to:

1) Identify some of the earliest video games to use sound and music,
2) Identify composers from this very early era,
3) Understand the basics of the NES and SNES sound production and how it impacted composers,
4) Understand the how the role of sound and music changed from the arcade to the living room.

3.1 The Earliest Uses of Music in Games: The Arcade

The earliest arcade games contained no sound whatsoever. Some very early games, such as *Pong* (1972) and *Computer Space* (1971) used very minimal sound effects, but no music or soundtrack. During the 1970s, when arcade games became popular, sound was primarily stored on large analog cassettes. These cassettes were expensive and prone to breakage, and thus unfavourable and very infrequently used in arcade cabinets. With the ability to use digital means such as computer chips to produce electrical impulses that result in sound waves, adding a musical or sound producing component became more practical. Sound was originally introduced, especially to the title screens of arcade games, as a means of luring customers to play the game. Some of the earliest games to use music or sound in their title sequences are *Gun Fight* (1975) and *Pac-Man* (1980). However, neither of these games had continuous musical soundtracks that looped once gameplay began. The first arcade game to contain a looping and musical soundtrack (not just sound effects) was *Space Invaders* (1978). While very musically limited (it consisted of the same four notes repeated over and over), the remarkable aspect of this soundtrack was that it responded to the player's actions. For example, the music speeds up if the player is about to lose the game, and slows down once the player begins to succeed. This is a very important component of game music and something that we will continue to explore later in the theoretical section of this book. The interactivity of video games is largely what separates them from other media, such as film. Therefore, music for interactive media should have its own unique characteristics.

The previous chapter discussed both synthesis and digital audio. Until 1980, all game sound was created using synthesis, at which point games began using limited amounts of digital audio (although synthesis would remain the primary method of sound generation for a long while). *Rally-X* (1980) was the first game to make use of digital audio samples. Other notable games are *Stratovox* (1980), which was the first game to use the synthesis of speech, and *Gyruss* (1983), the first game to use both synthesis and samples. At this point, the use of music in games was quite common, especially with the widespread implementation of FM synthesis in 1980. The first video game to use FM Synthesis was *Marble Madness* (1984). As we begin to study console music, it may seem as if arcades were more advanced for their time, and in many ways they were. Since arcades had large cabinets that were built differently for each game, different sound chips could be used depending on game need. Consoles had different sound production capabilities (which will be discussed below) that may appear more limited, and this is largely because they were physically smaller and standardized. Most early home computers (PCs) also contained more advanced computer chips (sound cards) than consoles. Early PCs had FM capabilities and therefore computer games had access to a larger sound palette. This will be discussed in more detail later as we explore 16-bit technology.

3.1.1 Early Consoles

Some of the earliest consoles were released during the late 1970s and early 1980s, such as the Atari 2600 (1977), the Intellivision (1979), and ColecoVision (1982). These were designed for home consumption and therefore marked a significant change in gaming - moving into the living room, rather than an arcade in an external social environment. They also represent the standardization of hardware. All of these systems had sound chips consisting of three channels: two additive synthesis channels and one noise generator. However, at this time, the state of game music was considerably different from what we are accustomed to today; composers were not often credited, and although the consoles had a very distinctive sound due to their sound chips, not all of the music was newly composed. Much of the music in these very early games consisted of reprogrammed public domain music. Dave Warhol is one of the pioneers in sound and music during this time, and worked on games for Intellivision, such as *Thin Ice* (1983). Warhol continued working in the field of game sound for several years, and later wrote software that could convert MIDI files (MIDI protocol is covered at length later in this section) into sound on old consoles, such as the Nintendo Entertainment System (NES).[6] These older consoles had distinct sound qualities due to their sound cards, and there are many contemporary performers that reproduce music using hacked versions of these classic consoles to recreate their unique sound. This performance practice is referred to as **Chiptunes**.

3.2 Nintendo Entertainment System (NES): Background and Sound Specifications

The success of arcade games, coupled with the significant decrease in cost of microprocessors, helped bring more advanced consoles into the home. While other home consoles existed prior to the release of the Nintendo Entertainment System (NES), such as those mentioned in section 3.1.1, we will begin our formal study of video game music with the Nintendo Entertainment System, because it has a large body of games and identifiable composers (composers were not always credited in early games). It was also on this console that music began to contain quite complex music and distinctly original thematic content. The NES was released worldwide between 1983 and 1987 (1983 release in Japan, 1985 in North America), and ended up being one of the most popular home consoles ever made, selling almost 62 million units.[7] Composers writing for the NES had to understand the technology they were composing for just as any composer of acoustic music needs to understand the instrumentation they are writing for and its capabilities. A piano, for example, has different sound qualities and capabilities than a flute, and therefore the composer has to approach it thusly. The NES contains five channels of sound output: 2 pulse wave generators, 1 triangle wave generator, 1 white noise channel, and 1 digital sample channel. Composers were limited therefore in timbral capabilities, and they were also limited in the amount of finer control they had over each channel. The pulse channels, for example, are capable of producing 16 different volumes, as well as pitch bend, but the triangle channel only has a singular volume setting. The noise channel also has 16 volume settings, and this channel was primarily used for percussive sounds. The audio sample channel contains 6-bit depth, and allows for 16 sampling rate settings between 4.2KHz to 33.5kHz. This channel was mostly used for very short audio clips and occasionally for sound effects. It is important

---

[6] See website of Real time Associates at: http://www.rtassoc.com/

[7] See link containing historical sales data of the NES here:
https://www.nintendo.co.jp/ir/library/historical_data/pdf/consolidated_sales_e1603.pdf

to keep these technological specifications in mind; composers for the NES did extremely remarkable things with these limited means.

3.3 Introduction to NES Composers

Here you will be introduced to some of the composers for the NES and their primary contributions to the history of video game music. This list is by no means complete, and you are encouraged to go out and seek other composers and music to study after completion of this text.

3.3.1 Nintendo Composers

Koji Kondo (b. 1961)

Koji Kondo was the first person hired by Nintendo for the purpose of creating musical compositions for the games (the third overall hire in game sound).[8] He is primarily known as the composer for the Mario and Zelda series, which contain some of the most universally recalled themes in video game music history. It is important to note that while Kondo was hired as a composer, his background is not in classical composition, and he cites many rock bands (and Rachmaninoff, a classical composer) as some of his influences.[9] Many composers of early video game music were more influenced by commercial popular music than film music, which would become a common influence of later composers. *Super Mario Bros* (1985) was Kondo's first major score, and has been incredibly successful: the theme song is a best-selling ringtone, has been sampled by many musicians, and has been performed at many concerts worldwide (and continues to be performed). Kondo is noted for his unique rhythmic style, an artefact of composing for the NES that persisted through his later works.

Hirokazu "Hip" Tanaka (b. 1957)

Hirokazu "Hip" Tanaka also worked for Nintendo following his application for a sound engineering job in 1980. Like Koji Kondo, he was heavily influenced by rock music, and actively a rock musician. However, he did study classical music as well from an early age. Tanaka was a student of electrical engineering, a skill he hoped he could apply to music, and did so successfully after joining Nintendo. Tanaka even contributed to the development of the audio hardware in the NES.[10]

---

[8] Otero, Joe. "A Music Trivia Tour With Nintendo's Koji Kondo." Imagine Games Network online magazine, Dec 10, 2014. http://www.ign.com/articles/2014/12/10/a-music-trivia-tour-with-nintendos-koji-kondo, accessed May 4, 2017.

[9] See "Koji Kondo interview" video at: https://www.youtube.com/watch?v=5ilJCerCucA

[10] Brandon, Alexander. "Shooting from the Hip: An Interview with Hip Tanaka."

Tanaka worked on a number of games, including the Donkey Kong series, several Mario spin-offs, and *Tetris* (1984). However, it is the *Metroid* (1986) soundtrack that represents one of his greatest contributions, as the success of the soundtrack led to the widespread desire for other video games and video game music composers to replicate it. Tanaka's approach to *Metroid* was also unique, as he tried to blur the lines between music and sound effects, and this is especially apparent in the opening sequence, where elements of the title music are emulating non-musical sounds, but remain components of the musical soundtrack. In this way, Tanaka was ahead of his time; the use of non-musical sounds are featured in many games of the post-HD generation, since composers have so much control over post-production.

3.3.2 Square-Enix Composers
Nobuo Uematsu (b. 1959)
A self-taught musician, Nobuo Uematsu's primary contribution is the extensive *Final Fantasy* collection. Uematsu never studied music formally, but played the piano from about the age of 10. He cites popular influences such as Elton John, Emmerson, Lake, and Palmer, Led Zeppelin, and many other progressive rock bands[11], but also world music, such as Celtic music.[12] Additionally, he is also a rock musician like Tanaka, and performed for several years in the rock group The Black Mages (who cover Final Fantasy songs) and later, the Earthbound Papas. Nobuo Uematsu is one of the most performed video game music composers worldwide, and his *Final Fantasy* soundtracks have multiple concert tours annually. These concerts represent some of the earliest examples of live performance of game music. Nobuo Uemastu could be considered one of the composers that has really helped to popularize video game music as a music to be listened to in its' own right, even outside of gameplay. He has received wide acclaim, and has been referred to as "legendary" and "Beethoven of video game music."[13]

Gamasutra online, Sep 25, 2002, http://www.gamasutra.com/view/feature/131356/shooting_from_the_hip_an_.php, accessed May 4, 2017.
[11] Dwyer, Nick. "Interview: Final Fantasy's Nobuo Uematsu," Red Bull Music Academy Daily, Oct 2, 2014, http://daily.redbullmusicacademy.com/2014/10/nobuo-uematsu-interview, accessed May 4, 2017.
[12] D, Spence, Schneider, Peer, and Dunham, Jeremy. "Nobuo Uematsu Interview." Imagine Games Network online magazine, July 9, 2004, http://www.ign.com/articles/2004/07/09/nobuo-uematsu-interview, accessed May 4, 2017.
[13] See position of "One-Winged Angel on Classic FM Hall of Fame at: http://halloffame.classicfm.com/2013/chart/position/3/

Koichi Sugiyama (b. 1931)

Koichi Sugiyama is primarily known for the *Dragon Warrior* (and later *Dragon Quest)* series. Unlike the previously mentioned composers, Sugiyama worked extensively in music prior to his career in video game composition, having composed for commercials and films, worked as a conductor, and provided musical arrangements. His influences are also considerably more classical, and he cites Baroque composers such as Bach and Handel as strong influences, as well as Classical composers Haydn and Mozart.[14] These classical roots are very identifiable in his music, and were beneficial on a system such as the NES: while many composers tended to use the available channels in standard lead, accompaniment, and bass set-up, he incorporated Baroque-inspired counterpoint in his music, for example. The NES was unable to produce a sound envelope (dynamic change over time), and therefore short notes were used often, and successfully. Baroque keyboard instruments such as harpsichord and organ also cannot easily produce these sound envelopes, which may explain why the Sugiyama's Baroque-style counterpoint was so effective for the NES.

3.3.3 Konami Group

The Konami group represents a group of composers who worked for the video game company Konami, originating during the NES era. Not all composers were credited in early video games, and this presents such an example. Currently there are some websites that identify the members, but at the time that the games were released, there was no information regarding who worked on the games' soundtracks. This makes it difficult to determine whether currently listed members of the club have composed for any NES games. The Konami Group is also nicknamed the "Konami Kukeiha Club", which literally translates to Konami Square Wave Club. Some of their more notable games were the *Castlevania* series, and *Genso Suikoden* (1995), but this group is considered responsible for essentially all of Konami's titles released for NES. Konami composers were credited later on, including in games released for the SNES.

3.3.4 Camcom Composers and Sound Team

Like many other Japanese companies during the 1980s, Capcom's sound department consisted of an in-house music staff comprising many sound teams that worked on games in groups. Capcom was also known for

---

14 See Koichi Sugiyama's Square Enix Music Online profile at:
http://www.squareenixmusic.com/composers/sugiyama/, accessed May 5, 2017.

having a strong presence of women as programmers, which persisted to later eras. This trait would later prove to be a large influence on major composer Yoko Shimomura deciding to work there.[15] Like the Konami group, not all of the Capcom composers were credited during the NES period, and sometimes composers were credited by monikers or pseudonyms. For example, Kumi Yamaga was credited as herself, but also as Yamachan and Jungle Kumi. Capcom's team-oriented departments and focus on in-house music staff persists through today, and some Capcom studios pride themselves as being some of the only remaining video game studios with in-house composers.[16]

3.4 Conclusion and Listening

Compositions for the Nintendo are for the most part timbrally and dynamically limited due to the constraints of the technology: recorded sound effects were used sparingly because of the low sampling rate, music was less continuously responsive to player input, and shorter loops were used that did not always have very smooth transitions. Nevertheless, composers found a way to create specialized soundtracks with very diverse music. Some characteristics and influences of each composer were mentioned above, but some general characteristics of NES music are as follows:

1) Mostly comprised of waveform synthesis (pulse, triangle), with samples used very sparingly,
2) Tended to be very rhythmically active, with lots of sound layering to add interest,
3) Limited timbral and dynamic palette,
4) Lots of arpeggiations and rapid (unplayable) passages - this is an artefact of the earliest video game music being handled by sound programmers, who intended to maximize sound while minimizing processing.

Below are several listening examples of soundtracks to NES games. I encourage you to seek out other NES music and discover how it compares to some of the works by composers mentioned above.

---

[15] Dwyer, Nick. "Interview: Street Fighter II's Yoko Shimomura." Red Bull Music Academy Daily Online, Sept 18, 2014, http://daily.redbullmusicacademy.com/2014/09/yoko-shimomura-interview, accessed June 12, 2017.
[16] Phone conversation with Capcom Vancouver employee, February 2016.

Koji Kondo: *Super Mario Bros.*, "Overworld Theme"
Koji Kondo: *Legend of Zelda,* "Theme"
Koji Kondo: *Super Mario Bros. 3,* "Theme"
Hirokazu Tanaka: *Metroid,* "Title Theme"
Hirokazu Tanaka: *Metroid,* "Brinstar"
Nobuo Uematsu: *Final Fantasy,* "Main Theme"
Nobuo Uematsu: *Final Fantasy,* "Battle Theme"
Koichi Sugiyama: *Dragon Warrior,* "Main Theme"
Koichi Sugiyama: *Dragon Warrior,* "Castle Theme"
Konami Group: *Castlevania,* "Main Theme"
Konami Group: *Castlevania,* "Boss Battle"

3.5 Super Nintendo Entertainment System (SNES): Background and Sound Specifications

The Super Nintendo Entertainment System (SNES) was released as a follow-up to the NES between 1990-1993 (1993 in North America). It was considerably more advanced than the NES, and contained its own audio chip, titled the Nintendo S-SMP. The SNES was capable of producing eight channels of 16-bit, 32kHz audio, a substantial increase from the NES, as well as a noise channel. An important new feature of the SNES was the possibility of sound envelope control, which gave composers the ability to change sound volume levels over time. This is different from the NES, where the volume level remains steady until a new note is played. This restriction is likely one of the reasons why so much of the musical output for the NES consists of relatively short notes and rhythmic patterns. Notes attacked on most acoustic instruments naturally decay over time, therefore a consistent volume envelope is perceived by the ear as unnatural. This control in the SNES represents a breakthrough in subtle dynamic expressivity. The other very significant change in the SNES generation was the ability of composers to compose and sequence (or put into software) music *away* from the console, and then hand the data for this already-composed music to a programmer who would add it to the game. This marks the beginning of the video game *composer* as a very separate concept from the video game *music programmer.*

3.6 SNES Composers

Here you will be introduced to some of the composers for the SNES and their primary contributions to the history of video game music. Just like the NES list of composers, this is not conclusive, and you are encouraged to go out and seek other composers and music to study after completion of this text. This section focuses primarily on new composers, although the works of previously mentioned composers are listed in the listening section - these works should be studied as well!

3.6.1 Nintendo Composers
Kenji Yamamoto (b. 1964)
Kenji Yamamoto worked for Nintendo as a composer as well as musical director. He began working for Nintendo in the late 1980s, and provided the soundtrack for a few NES games. He is primarily known, however, for contributing soundtracks to the Metroid series, because he took over for Hirokazu Tanaka as composer of *Super Metroid* (1994). Yamamoto's soundtrack contains his own personal style, but he manages to retain the overall atmosphere created by Tanaka in the original, including non-musical sounds in parts of the musical soundtrack. Like many of the other composers, his work, especially that from the Metroid series, is featured on several touring video game music concerts, most notably *Play! A Video Game Symphony.*[17]

3.6.2 Square-Enix Composers
Yasunori Mitsuda (b. 1972)
Yasunori Mitsuda was a protégé of Nobuo Uematsu, and has primarily composed the soundtracks to various Role-Playing Games (RPGs). He began composing music for his own video games while in high school, and held an intern position at Wolf Team in college under the tutelage of another video game composer, Motoi Sakuraba. He was hired by Square in 1992, although he contributed sound effects rather than music for the first two years. In 1994, Mitsuda threatened to quit Square, and was subsequently assigned the soundtrack to *Chrono Trigger* (1995).[18] The game saw incredible success and Mitsuda continued to compose several other soundtracks, including *Chrono Cross* (1999), a follow-up to *Chrono Trigger*. His music is also widely popular, being performed in orchestral concerts, and remixed by several bands and other groups, especially through the OverClocked ReMix community, which dedicated an entire album release to music from the Chrono series.[19]

Hiroki Kikuta (b. 1962)

---

[17] Now known as *re-Play: Symphony of Heroes*, found at: http://www.replay-symphony.com/, accessed May 5, 2017.
[18] Greening, Chris, "Yasunori Mitsuda Interview: His Life and Works." vgmo (Video Game Music Online), October 2005,
http://www.vgmonline.net/yasunorimitsudainterview/, accessed May 5, 2017.
[19] See information at: http://ocremix.org/album/7/chrono-trigger-chrono-symphonic, accessed May 5, 2017.

Hiroki Kikuta has a diverse background, and has worked as a composer as well as concept designer for video games. He graduated from university with a degree in Religious Studies, Philosophy, and Cultural Anthropology, and subsequently worked as an illustrator for Manga. He began to write music for anime and joined Square shortly thereafter.[20] Kikuta is also associated with RPG games like Mitsuda and Uematsu, and is primarily known for *Secret of Mana* (1993) and its' sequels. Kikuta also cites rock influence, and claims Pink Floyd is one of his greatest inspirations.[21] He also describes making music as being like "breathing" to him, stating that "music composing is a natural behaviour for me."[22] Kikuta's music shares many characteristics of Mitsuda's, such as very recognizable themes, prominent melodies, and culturally diverse musical influences. As we will see moving forward, these characteristics become consistent in the Japanese RPG (J-RPG) genre, and much such music retains certain qualities even as the technology continues to progress.

3.6.3 Namco Bandai Composers
Motoi Sakuraba (b. 1965)
Motoi Sakuraba began working at a developer called Wolf Team, which developed games for Namco, in 1989. It was here that Sakuraba tutored Yasunori Mitsuda as an intern. He started a serious musical career in college, and during this time he played in a progressive rock band (as we have seen thus far, progressive rock represents a large influence on many early game music composers). He has since composed for video games, anime, and television. Sakuraba also works as an arranger in addition to composer on several soundtracks. He is one of the most prolific video game composers, having worked on soundtracks in some capacity for over 160 games as of the writing of this book; this is in addition to his extensive work scoring for anime and television, and the production of his own solo albums. Sakuraba's game output is very diverse as well, including several RPG soundtracks (such as *Baten Kaitos* and *Eternal Sonata*) as well as arrangement projects for party games (such as *Super Smash Bros.*). This separates him from a lot of the other composers, who, while also prolific, tend to compose for similar genres.

---

[20] Greening, Chris, "Hiroki Kikuta profile." vgmo, modified March 21. 2014, http://www.vgmonline.net/hirokikikuta/, accessed May 5, 2017.
[21] See interview and profile information at:
http://www.rocketbaby.net/interviews_hiroki_kikuta_1.html, accessed May 5, 2017.
[22] Ibid.

3.6.4 Mega Man *Popularity and Inti Creates*

Several composers worked on the game *Mega Man* and then proceeded to join the company Inti Creates, which was created in 1996 by several ex-employees of Capcom. Inti Creates developed primarily games in the *Mega Man* series, and also produced several Mega Man albums with their in-house musicians. This group had several women composers, including Manami Matsumae, who worked at Capcom beginning in 1987, and Akari Kaida, who began working for Capcom in 1994. Music from Mega Man is some of the most extensively covered and remixed, and there are several video game music cover bands that are dedicated to performing or re-creating the music from the Mega Man franchise. *The Megas* and *Protomen* are two such bands. *Protomen* have been active since 2003, and have released several concept albums that are related to Mega Man. The music within the albums does not include direct covers, but music inspired by the music of Mega Man. *The Megas,* like *Protomen,* released covers as well as music inspired by or elaborating on Mega Man soundtracks. The group, which became active in 2008, added their own lyrics to their covers, and they even composed extra sections to the tracks. The approaches taken by *The Megas* and *Protomen* indicate that video game music can be re-visited by musicians in extremely creative and interactive ways, which is perhaps in the spirit of gaming culture.

3.7 SNES Listening

This section has given a very brief introduction to some of the composers of music for SNES games and their characteristic sounds. There are a plethora of games for the SNES, so it is encouraged to go and seek out other games, learn about their composers, and pay attention to how their sound compares (or doesn't compare) to the sound of the composers that have been covered so far. Generally some of the characteristics of the music for the SNES are:

1) Soundtracks are longer and more elaborate than soundtracks for the NES,
2) The timbres are beginning to sound more like orchestral instruments, and
3) The orchestration is fuller, and composers rely less on rhythmic interaction to make the soundtracks interesting (largely also due to the finer envelope control).

Kenji Yamamoto: *Super Metroid*, "Title Theme"
Kenji Yamamoto: *Super Metroid,* "Crateria"

Yasunori Mitsuda: *Chrono Trigger*, "Theme"
Yasunori Mitsuda: *Chrono Trigger*, "Time Circuits"
Hiroki Kikuta: *Secret of Mana*, "Theme"
Hiroki Kikuta: *Secret of Mana*, "Flight Theme"
Motoi Sakuraba: *Tales of Phantasia*, "The Dream Will Never Die"
Motoi Sakuraba: *Tales of Phantasia*, "Fighting of the Spirit"
Koji Kondo: *Super Mario World*, "Theme"
Nobuo Uematsu: *Final Fantasy VI*, "Terra's Theme"
Nobuo Uematsu: *Final Fantasy VI*, "Battle Theme"

3.8 Sega Genesis

The Sega Genesis was also a member of the 16-bit generation, although it was released two years prior to the Super Nintendo. Sega also released its own 8-bit system, the Sega Master System, but this was never very successful in North America, and the company achieved more success during that generation with its arcade games. Sega ported quite a few of their arcade games to the Genesis, and this represented a significant portion of the console's output. The Genesis had quite advanced sound capabilities, containing two separate sound chips: one chip contained three square wave channels, and the other chip contained an 8-bit sample channel and six FM synthesis channels. However, because these two sound chips required the programmer to use assembly language to program between them, programming sound for the Genesis was quite cumbersome. To reduce some of the coding complications, composers and music programmers relied on many pre-set sounds and instruments.[23] The Genesis, therefore, had extensive timbral capabilities, but the coding limitations prevented it from reaching its full musical potential at the time. The system did, however, make a substantial contribution in terms of its explorations with dynamic and interactive music (compare this to the SNES which relied more on already-composed material), and could be considered ahead of its time in that regard.

3.8.1 Toejam and Earl: Panic on Funkotron *(1992), John Baker*

Toejam and Earl contains one of the earliest examples of direct and intentional interaction between the player and the music in a game. There exists a mode within the game titled "jam out", in which the player is able to select a track from the soundtrack, and directly affect the music. During "jam out" mode, the player enters a special type of gameplay

---

[23] Collins, Karen. *Game sound: an introduction to the history, theory, and practice of video game music and sound design.* MIT Press, 2008, p. 40.

where they are in control of various percussive objects, and essentially "jam out" with the track. This is one of the first instances of interactive musical integration, and a precursor to some of the music-based video games, such as *Rock Band* and *Guitar Hero,* which would eventually become some of the most popular games during the 2000s.

3.8.2 Looney Toons, Desert Demolition *(1995), Sam Powell*

Desert Demolition involves the player selecting a Looney Toon as a player character, and the movements of that character result in sounds and musical motives. Each character has its own sound palette; therefore, choosing a particular character will result in a completely different soundtrack in comparison to other characters. The soundtrack uses a technique called Mickey Mousing, which is derived from film (often used in cartoons, such as Mickey Mouse, hence the name) and involves a direct link between the character's actions on screen and the occurring sounds.[24] This provides a very unique experience when the player has control over the character. This complete generation of sound by the player (and character) is a very interesting approach, and gives the player a completely different level of aural feedback, but it has yet to be implemented in a large collection of games. Player-generated music does exist in some more recent games, but generally with more subtle use, and realistic sound effects are much more commonly used.

3.9 Sega Genesis Listening

The sounds in Sega Genesis are very different from that of the NES, which was limited to mostly additive synthesis, and the SNES, which saw movement towards cinematic themes and away from heavily synthesized, rhythmic sound. The sound templates that were used for the Genesis to avoid excessive cumbersome coding resulted in a lot of sounds and instruments being reused, which did limit the diversity of sound, but gave the Genesis a distinct sound of its own. The music for games on the Genesis sounds much more like the earlier video game music, with quick rhythms and sound patterns that are not possible to play on traditional acoustic instruments. The Genesis also explored the interactive and player-responsive possibilities of sound more than its 16-bit counterpart. While the SNES was more advanced in many ways, with more advanced sound *quality,* the means with which the sound was produced meant that the SNES relied a lot more on longer composed pieces that looped and less on interactive sound.

---

[24] Wegele, Peter. *Max Steiner: Composing, Casablanca, and the Golden Age of Film Music.* Rowman & Littlefield, 2014, p. 37.

John Baker: *Toejam and Earl: Panic on Funkotron*
Looney Toons: Desert Demolition
Masato Nakamura: *Sonic the Hedgehog*, "Labyrinth"
Masoto Nakamura: *Sonic the Hedgehog*, "Scrab Brain Zone"

3.10 Developments in PC Sound

PCs tended to be more advanced in their sound production capabilities than home consoles. Most of the 16-bit and FM synthesis technology I will describe below was implemented in PCs long before equivalent console developments (1988-1992).

3.10.1 MIDI Standard

The development of the MIDI standard was one of the most important breakthroughs in music technology, as it marked the creation of a standard that could be replicated across all synthesizers. **MIDI protocol**, which stands for **Musical Instrument Digital Interface**, allows for these devices, such as musical instruments, controllers, and computers, to connect and communicate with each other via a specific type of messaging.[25] However, for the sake of video game music the most important aspect of MIDI is that it is essentially a series of control messages that tell a synthesizer what to do, and these messages are valid across a variety of devices. This standard enabled music to be sequenced away from and computers and then programmed into them later. However, not all sound cards (synthesizers) sound the same, so there tends to be minor differences in the sound between devices. Also, while MIDI was very advanced at the time, it contained only 127 different sounds, which by our standards today is relatively small. Nevertheless, the standard enhanced game music capabilities and provided an important tool for composers and sound programmers. However, it is crucial to remember that MIDI does not contain or transmit sound, only the data necessary to instruct a synthesizer to produce sound.

3.10.2 Hardware

Computer chips advanced at a faster pace in PCs than in home consoles, with the earliest very popular sound card for PC being released in 1986 by a Canadian company, AdLib Multimedia. This sound card was capable of producing 9 channels of FM synthesis and was based on the already-existing Yamaha YM3812. To place the release date of this chip in context with consoles, the NES was released between 1983-1987. The SNES was released in 1990, four years after this popular chip was

---

[25] See Electronic Music Interactive: http://pages.uoregon.edu/emi/32.php, accessed June 13, 2017.

released. Also remarkable about this sound card was that it came packaged with MIDI sequencing software called *Virtual Composer,* and an FM synthesis program called *Instrument Builder.* PCs at this time were therefore designed not only for gaming, but with consideration for the individual as composer as well. This was also made apparent by the computers' input and output arrangements; it was common for a gaming controller port to double as a MIDI input port (with adapter), and computers contained lines in for microphones and lines out to speakers.

3.10.3 iMUSE and Interactive Music
Another very important development that occurred during this time, which was invented at LucasArts in 1991, is the iMUSE system. This system was developed by Michael Land and Peter McConnell, and enhanced the interactive capabilities of game sound.[26] Video game music has always responded to player input in some way, but as the games became more complex, and the loops grew longer, musical transitions became complicated. Land and McConnell invented the system to enable smooth transitions in the music by creating a system that checked for gameplay conditions to be met at certain pre-specified checkpoints. This system varies from some of the other means of musical transitions, which often occur as a direct result of a player performing an action (such as entering a particular area). iMUSE revolutionized the way game music responded in real time, although advances such as this occurred more gradually on consoles.

3.11 Conclusion
Game music progressed substantially between the 1970s and the mid-1990s, both technologically and functionally. Technology and function drive the development of video game music, and by knowing the path through which both evolved, we gain a deeper understanding of why video game music sounds as it does. Technology became smaller in size, more accessible, faster, and contained more storage from the 1970s to the 1990s, enabling composers to create longer loops, more music, and use a wider variety of instrumental sounds. Capabilities for musical interactivity improved, and this interactive concept aids immersive sound in the later consoles. Functionally, game music began as an attempt to lure players with flashy sounds. This also evolved with the NES games containing music that sought to engage players and have catchy tunes. The 16-bit era saw some dabbling in interactive music, but the primary achievement of music functionality in this era is that of *individualism,* as

---

[26] Collins, Karen. *Game sound: an introduction to the history, theory, and practice of video game music and sound design,* p. 51.

game, character, and location themes became more unique and important.

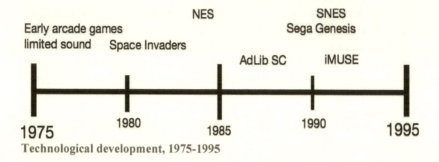

Technological development, 1975-1995

Chapter 4: Widespread Streaming Audio and the Move to Optical Discs

This chapter discusses the generation of video games beginning with the 32-bit consoles that contained the widespread use of streaming audio. We will see how composers gained more freedom from technological constraints, how responsiveness of sound to player actions improved, and how all of the advances in technology affected the general landscape of game music and sound. At this point, music was acknowledged to be a very important component of games, and opinions regarding its execution were developing. Unique styles of game music were also emerging. This was likely due to the fact that there were more video game studios in more diverse areas (we begin to see prominent video game development companies in many more locations besides Japan), and more genres of gameplay were becoming possible. Earlier Role-Playing Games, for example, all had distinctive stylistic traits in their soundtracks, but many of them were developed by the same company (Square) and a larger portion of them emerged from a very specific location (Japan). North American Role-Playing Games have a different style of game play, and thus, a different soundtrack paradigm. It is during this generation, therefore, that video game music undergoes a stylistic explosion; no longer can music be identified easily by its console or even by its genre. This is unprecedented; even with the diverse sounds available on the Super Nintendo and Sega Genesis, for example, it is not difficult to identify which console a given soundtrack on either system comes from.

4.1 Sega Saturn: Background and Sound

The 32-bit Sega Saturn was released in Japan in 1994 and 1995 in North America, and used CD-ROMs as game storage media. Sega developed its own Sega Custom Sound Processor, which had the capacity for 32 channels of 16-bit, 44.1kHz (CD quality) sound. However, the Saturn was somewhat limited in ability to utilize its hardware capabilities because of its design, which resulted in restriction of some of its memory. This was also because developers of this time were not accustomed to coding for devices with this design. The system was notably able to connect to the Internet for online play, a feature that Sega retained in later consoles. Online gaming was not widespread at the time, but has since proven to be one of the most important developments in gaming. The Saturn was popular, but its popularity was dwarfed by the release of the PlayStation, which is unfortunate, especially given that the Saturn was in many ways possibly more advanced. The decline in popularity was exacerbated by the lack of third party support, although some of the exclusive releases for the system have garnered their own nostalgic following, and the system as a whole, like many other Sega systems, has its own retroactive fan community. Therefore, while the system was released to mixed reviews, it has appeal to the retro gaming community in particular.

4.2 Sega Saturn: Games, Composers, and Listening

4.2.1 Nights Into Dreams *(1996), Various Composers*

Nights Into Dreams is an action game that follows two teenagers who enter a dream world. The game was praised for its graphics, as well as the flight handling within the game. A three-composer team, consisting of Naofumi Hataya, Tomoko Sasaki, and Fumie Kumatani developed the soundtrack. The soundtrack begins with a title song that has cinematic orchestral sound, with sweeping melodic themes. This type of title song would become more and more common in video games. The cinematic sound in *Nights Into Dreams* is different than most of the music for the Sega Genesis. The gameplay music, however, retains the quick, upbeat, pop/rock-inspired, synthesized sound that Sega composers have executed well in the past. The example below titled NiGHTS is the theme of the game; pay close attention when listening to this piece to how the orchestration, thematic material, and overall sound compare to other music for Sega. The other two examples are derived from in-game play. Listening:

> "NiGHTS"
> "Suburban Museum"
> "Growing Wings" (from Twin Seeds Level)

4.2.2 Panzer Dragoon *(1995), Yoshitaka Azuma*

The first instalment of the Panzer Dragoon series was released in 1995, and is a rail shooter game (or shoot 'em up) in which the player, along with other members of a team, rides a dragon and attempts to prevent a rival dragon from taking over. The dragon automatically progresses through the game and the player has a targeting reticle that they use to aim and shoot at enemies. The soundtrack, composed by Yoshitaka Azuma, reflects the gameplay of this genre and during this era: the music is fast-paced and upbeat, encouraging player engagement. It also carries stylistic traits of many other Sega games, including synthesized sounds and fast electronic beats. This high-energy music is likely a result of the gameplay, as rail shooters require the play to respond quickly and be

constantly on alert and engaged. There are some rock and pop influences, especially present in the main theme. However, the soundtrack is clearly distinct from other Saturn titles, such as NiGHTS, even though the stylistic tendencies consistent with Sega systems and described above are present.
Listening:

> "Opening theme"
> "Flight"
> "Departed Spirit"

4.2.3 Virtua Fighter (1994), Takayuki Nakamura

Virtua Fighter was ported to the Saturn from an earlier arcade game. The game is part of a series of fighting games created by Sega, and has had many further ports, spin-offs, and sequels. Like other fighting games, gameplay involves two combatants attempting to defeat one another two to three times, which results in one player's victory. The music in *Virtua Fighter*, like the other titles discussed for the Saturn, has heavy pop/rock influences, and very active beats. However, the structure of the soundtrack is quite different, since it consists only of several character themes. Unlike character themes in Role-Playing games, the themes in *Virtua Fighter* are not intended to evoke thematic and character development. They are instead intended to create player association between onscreen character and music while maintaining player engagement. This could also be a means of creating an analogue between the change of character and the change in sound (i.e., the characters and moves change, but not necessarily the gameplay and/or setting). In this sense, the music responds in the same manner as the visuals.
Listening:

> "Theme of Jacky"
> "Theme of Akira"
> "Theme of Kage"

4.3 PlayStation: Background and Sound Specifications

The PlayStation console was released in Japan in 1994 (1995 in North America), and was Sony's first gaming console. The PlayStation was immensely successful, being eventually the first console to ship 100 million units.[27] Like the Sega Saturn, the PlayStation used CD-ROM

---

[27] "Playstation 2 Breaks Record as Fastest Computer Entertainment Platform to

storage for its games. Therefore the PlayStation is also capable of CD-quality audio, although it has fewer available sound channels than the Saturn, containing 24 in total. The PlayStation has an interesting background, as it was initially intended to be a joint venture between Sony and Nintendo: Nintendo signed a contract in 1986 with Sony to develop a CD-ROM add on to their SNES. This plan fell through, and Sony eventually developed the PlayStation as their project.[28] Interestingly, one of the primary employees involved in this project, Ken Kutaragi, was originally inspired to begin this project because he was "dismayed by the [NES's] primitive sound effects" while watching his daughter play.[29] The PlayStation had excellent 3D graphics for its time, and was praised by Microsoft CEO Bill Gates, which is especially interesting since it was Microsoft who would eventually create one of Sony's main competitors, the Xbox. The console targeted an older audience, with teens and young adults as their primary player base, in contrast to the tween and preteen player base of Sega and Nintendo. Another important development of the PlayStation was in its ability to play back audio CDs; this would be retained across future CD-ROM systems, and in the later consoles, DVD (and Blu-ray) playback was possible. The success of the PlayStation, therefore, likely contributed to the decline in cartridge use.

4.4 PlayStation: Games, Composers, and Listening

The PlayStation has a diverse game library, and as such, the music for the PlayStation is also incredibly diverse. With the emphasis on graphics in this generation of console games, movie sequences in games began to appear, also known as FMVs (Full Motion Videos). These sequences encouraged music of a more cinematic style, as the accompaniment to these FMVs was not intended to loop, and was scored to follow specific visual events, much as a film soundtrack would. The gameplay music retained a lot of qualities of the music for SNES games, and was very individual depending on the overall qualities and features of the game. Another important development in PlayStation music is the increased use of pre-recorded audio, especially for FMV sequences. Often full-length songs with heavy post-production would be played back during these movie sequences. This is a very important indication of the time and

Reach Cumulative Shipment of 100 Million Units." Online resource, http://www.webcitation.org/5mEVIiLmD, accessed May 6, 2017.
[28] Swearingen, Jake. "Great Intrapeneurs in Business History." CBS News Online, updated Jun 17, 2008, http://www.cbsnews.com/news/great-intrapreneurs-in-business-history/, accessed May 6, 2017.
[29] Ibid.

concern that was put into game music by this time, and the emphasis placed on making game music excellent and memorable. The release of CD game soundtracks also became more widespread and popular outside of Japan, especially for long Role-Playing Games such as Final Fantasy. Game music was developing a market in its own right, as a listening genre, no longer just background music.

PlayStation Listening:

Nobuo Uematsu: *Final Fantasy VII,* "Aerith's Theme"
Nobuo Uematsu: *Final Fantasy VII,* "One-Winged Angel"
Michiru Yamane: *Castlevania: Symphony of the Night,* "Final Toccata"
Michiru Yamane: *Castlevania: Symphony of the Night,* "Requiem for the Gods"
Yasunori Mitsuda: *Chrono Cross,* "Time's Scar"
Yasunori Mitsuda: *Chrono Cross,* "Time's Grasslands"
Metal Gear Solid, "The Best is Yet To Come"
Metal Gear Solid, "Theme"

4.5 Nintendo 64: Background and Sound Specifications

The Nintendo 64 (N64) was released in 1996 in Japan, and boasted the most advanced processing technology of its generation. The Saturn and PlayStation only contained 32-bit processing, in contrast to Nintendo's 64-bit. Unlike the other consoles of its generation, however, Nintendo continued to use cartridges, which restricted the game storage capabilities considerably. The console was praised for its 3D graphics and processor, but compared to the PlayStation in particular, was limited in its game library. Without the larger storage capabilities of CDs, Nintendo 64 games could not incorporate FMVs as much as PlayStation games. This was not a drawback in gaming necessarily, but it did influence the music; fewer FMVs resulted in fewer tracks synced to picture (which encouraged cinematic style), and more music influenced by earlier game music, especially in titles such as Mario or Zelda that had NES or SNES releases. There are some very important musical developments in N64 games, with games such as *Donkey Kong 64* (1999) containing karaoke-style rap tracks, and *Legend of Zelda: Ocarina of Time* (1998) including a musical instrument as a key gameplay feature (this will be discussed at length later).

4.6 Nintendo 64: Games, Composers, and Listening

A lot of the sound and compositional characteristics of the music for Nintendo 64 games remained similar to those of the SNES, especially regarding style, but with better quality and resolution of sound, and more of a focus on the interactive, early game-inspired style of music, rather than the cinematic. However, this generation made the importance of video game music and its effect on the listeners and appeal very apparent. Many of the popular games for Nintendo 64 were sequels or follow-ups to previously released Nintendo games, which is likely why the stylistic characteristics remained so similar. At this point, distinctions in music for different genres also became clear; music for RPGs, for example, would have very different qualities than music for side scrolling (now 3D) action games. Genre-specific music will be discussed in more detail later on in this text. Following is a discussion of selected N64 soundtracks.

4.6.1 Zelda series

Ocarina of Time is examined for a couple of important reasons: first, it is another instalment by Koji Kondo in the Zelda series, which has been discussed and encouraged for listening in previous chapters. Additionally, the game contains a musical element as a key focus in the game. The main character, Link, is given an Ocarina, which he uses to transport himself to different time periods that he has previously visited. The player initiates use of the ocarina, and then uses specific buttons to play melodies that Link has "learned" over the course of the gameplay. Accurate completion of melodies results in Link being able to transport himself. This is interesting not only because an interactive musical element is so integral to the game, but also because of the impact it has upon the soundtrack. Many of the tracks in *Ocarina of Time* feature the sound of the ocarina, especially as a solo or melodic instrument. The follow-up to *Ocarina of Time, Majora's Mask* (2000) also included the use of the character's ocarina as an integral gameplay component. Listening:

> *Ocarina of Time*, "Title Theme"
> *Ocarina of Time*, "Enter Ganandorf"
> *Ocarina of Time*, Ocarina Melody: "Song of Time"
> *Ocarina of Time*, "Lost Woods"
> *Majora's Mask*, "Title Demo"
> *Majora's Mask*, "Fencing Grounds"
> *Majora's Mask*, Ocarina Melody: "Awake Sonata"

4.6.2 Grant Kirkhope, Rare Studios

Grant Kirkhope was born in 1962, in Edinburgh, Scotland. He worked for Rare studios before eventually becoming a freelance composer, where some of his more notable titles included *Donkey Kong 64* and *Banjo Kazooie* (1998). Kirkhope's soundtracks are characteristically fast-paced, very rhythmically driven, and tend to use specific instruments to evoke a character idea or concept. In *Banjo Kazooie,* for example, Kirkhope integrates a synthesized banjo sound, and other bluegrass style music, quite extensively, while conga drums are used in *Donkey Kong.* *Donkey Kong* also opens with a rap song. This song, DK rap, contains a repetitive hook, and adds a lyric track during playback, allowing the player to learn the words of the song. The gameplay tracks are very stylistically similar to those of other Nintendo games that evolved from their side scrolling counterparts (such as Mario), and serve to both engage the player, and provide an environment and reference point, which, in the case of *Donkey Kong*, is the jungle. Listen for the similarities and differences between the *Donkey Kong* and *Banjo Kazooie* soundtracks. Both soundtracks are very similar in musical style, with unique instrumentation that is depicts elements each game's setting. Listening:

> *Donkey Kong 64*, "DK Rap"
> *Donkey Kong 64*, "Monkey Smash"
> *Banjo Kazooie*, "Spiral Mountain"
> *Banjo Kazooie*, "Banjo Overture"

4.7 Conclusion, 32/64-bit

This generation contained a large advancement in the use of 3D (or pseudo-3D) graphics and gameplay, an indication and foreshadowing of the immersive aspect that would be so prominent in later generation games. The overall awareness of music's importance in games increased, with higher production quality, professionally recorded songs added to soundtracks, and soundtracks being released on CD as their own entity. Stylistic characteristics continued to persist through the generation, as many of the composers for specific games remained the same and the developments in technology primarily allowed for more realistic sounding instruments and larger storage. The biggest development of this generation was the capability of using streaming audio. This made long, pre-recorded audio tracks quite widespread in games, especially alongside FMVs. Previous storage capabilities simply wouldn't allow this, at least not at a sound quality that would be appropriate or pleasing to listen to. The same development can be seen in the visual domain of games at this time, as graphics improved and the FMV became prevalent throughout games, especially on the PlayStation. Streaming audio and the use of large pre-recorded audio pieces represent a means for scoring these sequences so that the music functions analogous to the visuals (linear songs alongside FMVs as opposed to looping media).

4.8 The next generation: DVD Optical Discs

The following generation saw primarily advancements in graphics, gameplay rendering, and sound quality. Part of this was due to advanced processing capabilities within the new consoles, but much was also due to the larger storage capabilities presented by the use of DVD optical disks. We will examine the PlayStation 2, the Xbox, the Nintendo GameCube and the Sega Dreamcast in this chapter. The PlayStation 2 and Xbox both opted for DVD-ROM as their storage method, while the GameCube and Dreamcast opted for mini-DVDs (GameCube), as well as mini CDs and a type of proprietary storage (Dreamcast). The GameCube and Dreamcast lagged considerably in success compared to the PlayStation 2 and the Xbox, and this use of different storage medium was a contributing factor, along with the lack of major third-party support for both consoles. Like a lot of consoles that had less popularity during their release, however, both the Dreamcast and the GameCube have generated retrospective interest, and many acknowledge that the Dreamcast especially, which was the first release of the four, was ahead of its time (like many other Sega consoles).

4.9 Nintendo GameCube

The Nintendo GameCube, released in 2001, represents Nintendo's first venture into optical disc storage media, although the console uses a proprietary mini-DVD rather than standard DVD-ROMS, and therefore, does not support DVD playback. The GameCube also has limited online gameplay support. The most popular games for the GameCube were the in-house follow-ups and sequels to many earlier games (such as Mario and Zelda), but there were quite a few successful third-party games, especially in the action/RPG genres. The primary drawback of many GameCube games, compared to their Xbox and PlayStation 2 counterparts, remains the storage method: Nintendo mini DVDs store about 1.5 GB of data, compared to over 8GB of data possible on the DVD-ROMS that are used in the PS2 and XBox. This had an impact on both the quality of graphics as well as the scope of the games. The Nintendo GC, therefore, did not live up to the PS2 and Xbox in widespread popularity. Music for GameCube tends to be higher resolution and higher quality than music in N64, with genre-specific stylistic similarities.

4.9.1 Legend of Zelda: The Wind Waker (2002)

Like *Ocarina of Time*, this game also involves direct interaction with a musical object as an integral component to the gameplay, although in this game this object is a baton called a Wind Waker, which the player has to use to conduct in the game. While the main character, Link, is conducting, music plays in rhythm with his conducting patterns. The soundtrack retains a lot of qualities of previous Zelda games, including lyrical, upbeat melodies and heroic themes. Also notable is the amount of wind instruments used in the game, including flute-like instruments and bagpipes; which seem to have become a trademark for Zelda games. *The Wind Waker* takes place on a group of islands, which is a different setting than other Zelda games, and the music reflects this setting by including Celtic instruments, Mediterranean guitar, and castanet sounds (all sounds from island regions). This can also be observed in the titling of tracks, like "Pirates".
Listening:

> "Title"
> "The Legendary Hero"
> "Pirates"
> "Dragon Roost Island"

4.9.2 Baten Kaitos Origins (2006), Motoi Sakuraba

Baten Kaitos Origins is a Role-Playing Game that used a unique card storage system for character, equipment, and attack elements. The game was a follow-up to an earlier Baten Kaitos game, released in 2003, and both had soundtracks composed by Motoi Sakuraba. The game was released late in the life cycle of the GameCube, in 2006, and did get a warm reception from critics and players, although this was likely overshadowed by the release of the Wii console later that year. Like a lot of RPGs, *Baten Kaitos Origins* contained a pop ballad-style song that would be the main theme of the game, titled *Le Ali Del Principio*. The lyrics to this theme were written by Sakuraba's wife, and the song was performed by his (then) 9-year old daughter.[30] There are several rock and pop influences throughout the game (such as in "Chaotic Dance 2", see below), and even use of side effects alongside music (as in "Ruins"). General stylistic traits of music for RPGs of this era, including lengthy

---

[30] Sakuraba, Motoi. *Baten Kaitos Origins OST*, CD liner notes.

melodies, can also be observed in the soundtrack ("Hometown of the Past").
Listening:

> "Le Ali Del Principio"
> "Chaotic Dance 2"
> "Ruins"
> "Hometown of the Past"

4.10 Sega Dreamcast

The Sega Dreamcast was the first release of its generation, hitting shelves in Japan in 1998, almost three years prior to the PS2. The Dreamcast was Sega's final console. While not as successful as its generational counterparts, the Dreamcast was considered by many to be ahead of its time; it was actually the first console to contain a built-in modem, easing online play. The Dreamcast faltered because it attempted to lower costs at the expense of technical capabilities, a difficult decision when other consoles were opting for ever-increasing graphic realism.[31] The system also had limited third-party support, although many of the games that were released for the Dreamcast are gaining recognition in the present. Also, much like the GameCube, Sega opted for mini discs, and its own proprietary storage medium, the GD-ROM. These proprietary media were intended to restrict piracy, but had limited storage space, much like the GameCube discs (1GB for the Dreamcast's GD-ROM). This also meant that the Dreamcast could not also function as a DVD player, a drawback shared by the GameCube. This was a desirable feature at the time, due to the high price of standalone DVD players.

4.10.1 Phantasy Star Online *(2000)*, Hideaki Kobayashi and Fumie Kumatani

Phantasy Star Online represents one of the first console-based online multiplayer games, and the game features both online and offline modes of play. *Phantasy Star Online* is a Role-Playing Game that differs slightly from many others of its genre because it uses a real-time combat system, rather than a turn-based action-selection system. This means that the gameplay is much faster-paced and immediate, rather than involving selection of actions through a list of text. The player, as in many computer-based RPGs of the time, selects a type of character (based on

---

[31] McFerran, Damien. "Hardware Classics: Sega Dreamcast." Nintendolife online, Apr 16, 2015, http://www.nintendolife.com/news/2015/04/hardware_classics_sega_dreamcast, accessed May 6, 2017.

fighting style) that can be customized in appearance and ability. The story of the game follows this character as they examine locations for a habitable place to relocate a civilization. The game was a substantial jump towards a completely new type of gameplay on consoles, and was immensely successful, eventually being ported to many other systems, including the GameCube and Xbox. This type of online gameplay was, until this point, primarily available on personal computers. Since the game has a science fictional and space-based setting, the soundtrack contains a lot of synthesized sounds, evoking futuristic, space-like environments. Additionally, the music becomes much more ambient and atmospheric in a lot of areas. This is perhaps in response to the type of gameplay expected of online games: generally longer (lasting weeks, months, or years, rather than a few days), and with more objects and actions to visually keep track of, especially when playing with a large group or at a high difficulty. Compare the qualities and style to the soundtracks we have explored for other RPGs, such as *Final Fantasy*, or *Chrono Trigger*. Some elements of this soundtrack are similar to the RPG genre, and some are different, and reflective of the online environment and the differing gameplay style.
Listening:

> Hideaki Kobayashi: "A Song for Eternal Story"
> Hideaki Kobayashi: "Mother Earth of Dishonesty Part I"
> Hideaki Kobayashi: "Growl, from the Depths of the Earth"
> Fumie Kumatani: "Kink in the Wind and the Way, Part I"
> Fumie Kumatani: "From Seeing the Rough Wave"
> Fumie Kumatani: "Can Still See the Light"

4.11 PlayStation 2/Xbox

The PlayStation 2 and Xbox were the most popular systems of the DVD-ROM generation. I discuss them together for a couple of reasons: 1) they use the same storage medium, 2) many games were released on both (in addition to PC/Mac), and 3) the capability of the hardware is quite similar, leading to very similar quality in graphics and sound. The games library did differ somewhat for the consoles, and exclusive titles for the Xbox tended to be primarily first or third person shooters, while the PlayStation 2 exclusives were mostly third-person action games or RPGS. The PlayStation 2 outsold the Xbox worldwide, but the Xbox had several of its own games and technology that had quite an impact, which was influential to both gameplay and game sound. The most notable difference in sound technology was Xbox's support of the Dolby Digital 5.1 system during interactive playback; previous systems were only capable of using Dolby Digital during cut scenes.[32] This contributed to the depth of high-action content games such as First Person Shooters available on the Xbox. Players need to be aware of enemies that are surrounding them in such games, and sound plays an important role in establishing event localisation cues. Therefore, interactive surround sound is valuable during FPS and other fast-paced games. While the interactive surround sound was primarily used for sound effects, it encouraged other development in interactive game sound, and games such as Halo (discussed at length later in this text) were extremely innovative in this regard.

4.11.1 Silent Hill Series, Akira Yamaoka

Silent Hill is a series consisting of several horror-themed games, the first of which was released in 1999 for the PlayStation. The game, which is set in a fictional American town, tried to evoke a more Hollywood-style environment in order to draw more North American gamers. *Silent Hill* (1999) is a psychological thriller, inspired by literature, unlike many of the zombie-themed horror games that are more overt and fast-paced, often incorporating elements such as jump scares. The gameplay type in *Silent Hill* is third-person action and involves a lot of puzzle-solving elements. The series uses a lot of symbolism in the games, a feature common to both literature and American psychological thriller films. This adds another layer to the game, although a subtle and understated one (especially during a period in which games are becoming increasingly more saturated with graphics and action). The music effectively sets this game, containing subdued themes, limited timbres and instruments, and delicate use of sound processing. Akira Yamaoka effectively illustrates the solitude and unsettling nature of these games. Listening:

> *Silent Hill*, "Theme"
> *Silent Hill 2*, "Laura's Theme"
> *Silent Hill 2*, "A World of Madness"
> *Silent Hill 3*, "Heads No. 2"
> *Silent Hill 3*, "Dance With the Night Wind"

---

[32] "The Xbox Video Game System from Microsoft to Feature Groundbreaking Dolby Interactive Content-Encoding Technology." Online press release archival, http://web.archive.org/web/20060219162524/http://www.dolby.com/assets/pdf/press_releases/841_co.pr.0104.xbox.pdf, accessed May 6, 2017.

4.11.2 God of War (2005), Various Composers

God of War was released for PlayStation 2 in 2005, and used ancient Greek mythology (a loose depiction thereof) as its setting and narrative. The third-person action game followed the story of Kratos, who attempts to avenge himself against Ares, the God of War, after he was tricked into killing his own family.[33] The gameplay involves hack-and-slash type combat, fast-paced action, and very lofty, titan-esque themes. The soundtrack adequately portrays this in scope, style, and sound team size - several composers worked on it, including Gerard K. Marino, Ron Fish, Winifred Phillips, Mike Reagan, Cris Velasco, Winnie Waldron, and Marcello De Francisci. The music in *God of War* uses Greek and Ancient Near Eastern-associated instruments to depict setting, and incorporated some melodies referencing ancient Greek music (especially in the use of chromatic half steps followed by larger musical leaps). There is also a heavy low brass, string, and choir presence throughout, giving the soundtrack a more cinematic and grandiose presence. Note that while the music is incredibly dense in its orchestration, it is actually not as fast-paced and energetic as some previous soundtracks for such action-oriented games. We will begin to see more frequently that as graphics and sound effects become more realistic, the music moves away from the hyper-rhythmic style so popular in early games.
Listening:

> "Kratos and the Sea"
> "Splendor of Athens"
> "End Title"

4.11.3 Final Fantasy XII (2006), Various Composers

Final Fantasy games are renowned for their lengthy and well-crafted soundtracks, and as we learned previously, Nobuo Uematsu remains one of the most popular composers of video game music. *Final Fantasy XII* marks the first instalment of the series with a soundtrack not composed by Uematsu, as he had departed Square to work independently at this time. A three-member team consisting of Hitoshi Sakimoto, Hayato Matsuo, and Masaharu Iwata composed the soundtrack, although Nobuo Uematsu made a contribution as well. Like other Final Fantasy soundtracks, it remains notable for its memorable themes and melodic content. Also like many other Japanese Role-Playing Games (J-RPGs), especially in the post-PlayStation era, it contains a full-length pop song, which often serves to help promote the game. This song, "Kiss Me

---

[33] *God Of War*, Sony Computer Entertainment, 2005.

41

Goodbye", (English title) was performed by Angela Aki and composed by Nobuo Uematsu. It became a major hit in Japan, although it never saw similar pop chart success in North America. Hitoshi Sakimoto composed the majority of the soundtrack for the game, and noted how difficult it was to follow in Uematsu's footsteps, opting out of extensive interaction with Uematsu while he was composing to avoid his music sounding too much like Uematsu's.[34] The result was a soundtrack that retained some of the key qualities of J-RPG soundtracks, but that was substantially different than the previous Final Fantasy titles.
Listening:

> Hitoshi Sakimoto, "Theme of *Final Fantasy XII*"
> Taro Hakase and Yuji Toriyama, "Hope" (ending credits)
> Nobuo Uematsu, "Kiss Me Goodbye"

4.11.3 Halo: Combat Evolved (2001), Martin O'Donnell and Michael Salvatori

Halo was perhaps one of the most influential of the Xbox-exclusive titles, eventually resulting in many sequels, spin-offs, and fan media, including both authorized novels and fan fiction. *Halo* was widely praised as being one of the best first-person shooter games available for a home console at that time. The game follows the story of John, or Spartan-117, a super soldier defending the planet from a race of aliens known as the Covenant.[35] Throughout the game, 117 receives instructions and feedback from an Artificial Intelligence (AI) companion, Cortana. The music was composed by Martin O'Donnell and Michael Salvatori. The *Halo* theme itself has also become iconic, consisting of a choir opening reminiscent of Gregorian chant, followed by the action packed drum and string sequence. Something very notable regarding the *Halo* soundtrack is the use, reuse, and repurposing of a singular theme throughout the game. Elements from the title theme recur in the music from every level, but the context is changed. O'Donnell achieves this by using techniques such as changing the instrumentation, the arrangement, or fragmenting components of the theme. This musical quality persists even in the *Halo 2* soundtrack (and later sequels), and also has an impact on other games. This use of theme is discussed at length in section two of this text.
Listening:

---

[34] Interview with Hitoshi Sakimoto. *Final Fantasy XII Collector's Edition Bonus DVD* (DVD). Tokyo: Square Enix. 2006.
[35] *Halo: Combat Evolved*, Bungie, 2001.

"Title Theme"
"Brothers in Arms"
"Perilous Journey"
"Covenant Dance"

4.12 Reception of Video Game Music

Game music during this time became more obviously important: more complete and individual soundtracks emerged during the 8-bit era and through the 16-bit era, and during the 32-bit era game soundtracks were regularly released on CD for individual purchase. Some of these soundtracks were so large in scope that they contained over one hundred tracks. This indicates that in this short period of time (only slightly over a decade), game music had progressed from being primarily implemented to lure arcade customers, to becoming a genre of music that could be listened to on its own outside of gameplay. By the early HD generation, there were several touring symphonic concerts dedicated to video game music, bands dedicated to remixing video game music, and many other such performance groups.

4.12.1 Video Game Music Performances

Video game music has become an important part of symphonic performance in the last decade and a half, and the reception of video game music in the concert hall is well documented.[36] Video game music symphonies tend to be extremely well attended, and this has generated discussion surrounding the importance of video game music concerts to the public interest, and as a result, the fiscal health, of many symphonies.[37] Audience participation and involvement tends to be different at video game music concerts as well. Traditional classical music concerts generally involve attendees dressing up semi-formally or formally, and sitting in the concert hall without talking, clapping, or otherwise interacting with the musicians until the ends of pieces. Attendees at video game concerts often dress up in the costume of their favourite character, contrary to the potentially restrictive formal wear one would wear to an opera. The audience is encouraged to clap and cheer during pieces, and

---

[36] see videos such as https://www.youtube.com/watch?v=ja5h3Y2KDHc, which includes Nobuo Uematsu playing the flute, and this video, https://www.youtube.com/watch?v=rD0p7EfMa9U, titled "We Love Video Game Music", accessed May 15, 2017.
[37] Needleman, Sarah E. "How Videogames are Saving the Symphony Orchestra." The Wall Street Journal online, Oct 12, 2015, http://www.wsj.com/articles/how-videogames-are-saving-the-symphony-orchestra-1444696737, accessed May 15, 2017.

some concerts even include active audience participation. This makes the concert a much more interactive experience than traditional symphony concerts, and perhaps more appealing to the younger generations that are so accustomed to interactive technology and media. Video game symphony performance became widespread and popular primarily during the 2000s, but there were a few video game music concerts that preceded this. The *Orchestral Game Music Concerts* began in 1991, and ran until 1996. These concerts occurred in Tokyo and included performances of music from various video games. Germany followed this in 2003 with *Symphonische Spielemusikkonzert* (Symphonic game music concerts), a series inspired by the *Orchestral Game Music Concerts* that would become the first of its kind outside of Japan. This concert was intentionally held alongside other game industry events, such as the Game Convention (GC), to encourage attendance. These early video game concerts, however, were geographically limited (Tokyo and Germany) and did not include touring or other widespread repeated performance. This would not occur until the mid-2000s, when several game music symphonies began, most of which now tour nationally or worldwide. Some of the more common video game symphonies include *Final Fantasy: Distant Worlds, Play! A Video Game Symphony,* and *Video Games Live.*

4.12.2 Remixes - OverClocked

There are also several bands dedicated to the remixing, covering, and re-working of video game music. This is influenced by the popularity of game music, and indicates that game music is an ideal genre to perform and remix. OverClocked, which was launched in 1999, provides a unique platform for users to experience remixes and reworkings of video game music. The website describes itself as an "organization dedicated to the appreciation and promotion of video game music as an art form".[38] The works uploaded are called "ReMixes" (rather than re-mixes or covers) because the founder, David W. Lloyd, imagined them to be collections of reworkings and re-arrangements of existing game music, rather than alterations to master tracks (and therefore not truly remixes).[39] This website has resulted in the dissemination of a multitude of fan-made works, including more than 3000 ReMixes by more than 900 contributors. Lloyd's intent was that the site would be a non-commercial platform, but contributor attribution is required, indicating the

---

[38] From the Overclocked remix website, www.ocremix.org/info/AboutUs, accessed May 15, 2017.
[39] Bandit, Cat. "To OC or Not to OC, That Is the ReMix", Hyper, March 2014, pp. 6–10.

importance the site places on artistic integrity. Over 105 albums of these remixes have been released as of 2016.[40] Another interesting feature is the online community and forums, which provide a type of "peer review" platform, as users can comment on other ReMixes. The ReMixes are generally well received even among those in the game music industry, and many composers have praised the ReMixes of their works. Some video game composers have even contributed to the database, including Jeremy Soule, who provided a remix to *Final Fantasy VI*, and George Sanger, who in 2002 was the first industry game composer to provide a remix. Additionally, several ReMixers have gone on to working in the video game music industry, including Dain Olsen (*Dance Dance Revolution*), Jillian Aversa (*Civiliation IV*), Andrew Aversa (*Monkey Island 2 Special Edition*), Jimmy Hinson (*Mass Effect 2*), and Danny Baranowsky (*Super Meat Boy*). Therefore, OC Remix is not just an important display of the general public's enthusiasm for game music; it has also provided a platform for independent musicians who have a passion for game music to be noticed.

4.13 Cinematic or Interactive?

During this period we also begin to see a divergence in aesthetics, however limited, between sound that is derived from cinematic styles and sound that retains "video game" sound - essentially, the qualities that made early game music unique and evolved from those traditions. Even in the High-definition (HD) consoles (which will be discussed later), composers had to decide between live instrumental sound and sampled (synthesized) sound, depending on how interactive they wanted the sound to be, or if they wanted to execute passages that are unplayable by live instruments. Because MIDI information does not contain any sound - only 1s and 0s that instruct the sound chip which sound to make, it is more adaptable to interactive input. Recorded audio still has the limitation that once the sound is played, it cannot be modified. Changes in speed and other sound properties are becoming more possible with technological advantages, however, and advancements continue to be made. The type of synthesized and interactive sound became an aesthetic that many composers sought after, and not merely because of technological limitations - potential had grown beyond those limitations and using such music was an aesthetic choice. There was also a trend emerging, however, in which video game music began to sound more like film music, or at least as if it was inspired by film music. One of the

---

[40] See https://ocremix.org/albums/, accessed June 12, 2017.

pioneering composers of the cinematic style of composition was the American composer Jeremy Soule.

4.13.1 Jeremy Soule and Legacy

Jeremy Soule was born in the Midwestern United States in 1975. He is one of the first extremely successful western composers of video game music, and one of the first American composers to contribute heavily to the Role-Playing Game genre.[41] Soule started working for Square in 1994 after sending a demo tape to both LucasArts and Square. He has substantial classical influences, including Debussy (harmony), Wagner (operas), and Mozart (form). Soule is primarily known for the *Elder Scrolls* series, and *Guild Wars,* although he has written the soundtracks to many titles and has a continuously prolific output. Jeremy Soule's music reflects stylistic traits by other RPG composers such as Nobuo Uematsu, but has heavy cinematic influences, which are especially apparent in the thematic content and orchestration of his music. Listening:

> *Elder Scrolls III: Morrowind,* Nerevar Rising
> *Elder Scrolls III: Morrowind,* Bright Spears, Dark Blood
> *Elder Scrolls III: Morrowind,* Shed Your Travails
> *Guild Wars II,* Overture
> *Guild Wars II,* Call of the Raven

4.14 Conclusion

While there were breakthroughs in technology during this generation, including the use of ROMs, more storage space, and faster processing, the music did not undergo any major transformations as large in scope as the change between the 8-bit and 16-bit generations, for example. The resolution of graphics evolved, and visuals became more realistic, therefore the advancement of sound was a logical course of action, leading to more pre-recorded music and orchestral instruments (live and sampled). Video game music became a listening medium in its own right during this generation; video game soundtracks began to be consistently released on CD or for download, and the video game orchestra developed and gained substantial popularity. Video game music was consistently performed at events, and game music stood a category in video game awards. Very distinct styles were emerging, and composers could now

---

[41] "Interview with Composer Jeremy Soule at Play! San Jose." Music4games online archive, June 6, 2007, http://web.archive.org/web/20080620051533/http://www.music4games.net/Features _Display.aspx?id=145, accessed May 6, 2017.

choose freely between pre-recorded audio and MIDI sounds for aesthetic preference, rather than as a result of technical limitations. The focus continued to be more immersive, realistic sound, which would continue to the next generation. However, as the sounds became more immersive, with some even generated live during gameplay, sound effects began to take precedence, and the memorable, catchy, melodies of the early games began to fade and give way to more cinematic sound or atmospheric sound in many cases. This will be explored more in the next section, as we begin to examine the high definition generation.

Chapter 5: The HD Generation and Beyond

This chapter examines the music and sound of games of the generation of consoles that began to use High Definition (HD) graphics and sound. It also examines how the rise of mobile gaming, networked gaming, and online gaming has shaped music sound in games. There are two large technological developments that occur during this time, the first being the hardware and storage media (HD-DVD, Blu-Ray). The second, which is more indirectly related to the development of consoles, is the change in social interaction and media dissemination as a result of online platforms such as Facebook and YouTube. This change impacted console evolution and encouraged the developers to integrate more online capabilities and multiple functions. The accessibility of game development equipment also expanded, and, coupled with crowd funding websites, led to an increase in independently produced games and applications. The end result was an increase in extremely high quality and high definition AAA games as well as an increase in small-scale independent games, many of which had appeal to retro gaming crowds or to casual and non-hardcore gamers.

5.1 The Early HD Consoles (PS3, Xbox 360, Wii)

The first-generation HD consoles were released in 2006, and consist of the PlayStation 3 (PS3), Xbox 360, and the Nintendo Wii (a member of the generation but the only console not to transition to HD graphics). The main developments in gaming during this generation were improved graphic resolution, vastly improved storage space, improved sound resolution, and console multi-functionality. All of the consoles had online capabilities. This is an extension of early services such as Xbox Live, which started out with limited game support and became eventually immensely popular. With the release of the Xbox 360, the service was expanded to be functional with nearly all games, and gave users the option to download games, create avatars, download applications which are unrelated to gaming (you can, for example, watch Netflix and YouTube on Xbox 360). Like many other electronic devices of this time, such as phones that began to double as cameras and Internet browsers, consoles were becoming capable of much more than just gaming.

5.1.1 Wii

The Wii was technically the least advanced of its generation, opting not to include HD graphic capabilities, and investing more research and development resources into innovative gameplay. The Wii changed user interaction with games by integrating a motion-sensing controller, which was titled the WiiMote. This controller enabled players to use motion to perform physical gestures to play games. Nintendo recognized that while graphics had continually improved over the last two decades, the interaction design within games remained essentially the same, and they had begun working on a motion sensing controller as early as 2001.[42] Therefore, while the Wii was less advanced than its generational counterparts in terms of graphics, the WiiMote actually represented a major breakthrough in gaming interaction design. The Wii, like the 360 and PS3, also had online capabilities and an integrated online store, called the Wii Marketplace, which allowed users to shop for apps, downloadable games, and more. The WiiMote had a small speaker embedded into the controller, which was not used to playback music, but rather played back sound effects for aural feedback during gameplay. This type of feedback is similar in functionality to in-game sound effects, and possibly even represents an extension of the vibration and haptic feedback in many recent controllers (like the PS2 DualShock, etc). While the WiiMote and motion-sensing gaming never became popular in hardcore game titles, it was extremely popular for casual and party games, and represented the beginning of an era that would see continued innovation of user interaction design.

5.1.2 Wii Listening

The Legend of Zelda: Twilight Princess (2006) was the first title to be released on the Wii console in 2006. The game does make use of the motion sensitive controllers, although much of the control design is derived from prior iterations of the series, and simply extended to include the motion control.[43] Koji Kondo served as music supervisor for the game, but he did not write the soundtrack, and Toru Minegishi and Asuka Ohta were the primary composers for the game. The vision for the music originally involved the use of a large orchestra. This idea never came to fruition, partially because Kondo did not agree that the implementation of an orchestra would make a large difference, and also because sequenced music made interactivity more feasible.[44] While increased interactivity of music had been an important feature of

[42] Rothman, Wilson. "Unearthed: Nintendos Pre-Wiimote Prototype." Gizmodo online, Aug 29, 2007, http://gizmodo.com/294642/unearthed-nintendos-pre-wiimote-prototype, accessed May 6, 2017.

[43] Kaluszka, Aaron. "*The Legend of Zelda: Twilight Princess.*" Nintendo World Report online, Jan 11, 2007, http://www.nintendoworldreport.com/review/12702/the-legend-of-zelda-twilight-princess-gamecube, accessed May 6, 2017.

[44] Casamassina, Matt. "*The Legend of Zelda: Twilight Princess* Review." Imagine Games Network online, Nov 17, 2006, http://www.ign.com/articles/2006/11/18/the-legend-of-zelda-twilight-princess-review-2, accessed May 6, 2017.

previous Zelda games (such as *Ocarina of Time*), this did not result in entirely good reviews for the music, with one reviewer stating that "the MIDI tunes are passable, but they lack the punch and crispness of their orchestrated counterparts."[45] *Twilight Princess* also makes extensive use of the WiiMote speaker, using it to playback fighting sound effects and trademark chimes upon secret discovery.
Listening:

> "Theme"
> "Opening"
> "Ordon Village"
> "Hyrule Field"

5.1.3 Xbox 360
The Xbox 360 was also released in 2006, although with significantly more advanced hardware, and a higher retail price than the Wii. It also focused heavily, like the Wii, on an online component, with live multiplayer being one of the main features of the console. Xbox Live was substantially upgraded and expanded over the original Xbox version, and nearly all 360 games contained Xbox Live support. Downloadable content for games, arcade games, and applications was an important feature, and the ability to download and use extra media such as music, movies, and other software contributed to the Xbox 360's establishment as a multifunctional device. There were multiple hook-ups and peripherals for the 360, and one of these devices was the Xbox Kinect, a motion-sensing camera that a player interacted with during certain games. The Kinect, much like the WiiMote, never gained popularity as an interface for hardcore games, but did contribute to the rise of dance and movement-based games, and represented once again the desire to innovate gaming interaction design. The Xbox 360 was not the highest selling console of its generation, but did help further popularize the Xbox brand. One significant drawback of the 360 was that it incorporated an HD-DVD player rather than Blu-Ray (the PS3's medium), and HD-DVDs ended up becoming discontinued. This was not necessarily a lack of foresight on part of Xbox, however, since at the time it was yet undetermined which storage medium would become preferred.

5.1.4 Xbox 360 Listening
The Xbox 360 had extremely immersive sound, and very high sound quality, partially due to the increases in processing and storage, and also due to the interactive Dolby Digital 5.1 capabilities. Previously discussed

---

[45] Ibid.

in regards to computer games was the link between FPS games and the rise in surround sound, and the Xbox 360 is no exception. The console continued to produce many exclusive titles of the FPS and Third Person Shooter (3PS) genres, as well as Stealth Games. All of these games are improved substantially by interactive surround sound and sound localisation cues. Games such as these include advanced HUDs (Heads up Display) to aid the player in keeping track of information such as ammo, current weapon inventory, and maps. Therefore, spatialization of sound gives another level of feedback to the player. While most of this is accomplished with sound effects, the spatial placement and volume of music can also cue the player to both directionality and distance from certain objects. The 360 also expanded its RPG library, continuing to release traditional Xbox titles such as The Elder Scrolls series while also supporting J-RPGs such as *Eternal Sonata* (2007) and *Lost Odyssey* (2007).

Listening:

> Kevin Reipl: *Gears of War*, "Main Theme"
> Kevin Reipl: *Gears of War*, "Fish in a Barrel"
> Garry Schyman: *Bioshock*, "Main Theme"
> Garry Schyman: *Bioshock*, "Cohen's Scherzo No. 7"
> Nobuo Uematsu: *Lost Odyssey*, "Main Theme"
> Nobuo Uematsu: *Lost Odyssey*, "A Mighty Enemy Appears"
> Motoi Sakuraba: *Eternal Sonata*, "Pyroxene of the Heart"

5.1.5 PlayStation 3

The PlayStation 3 incorporated Sony's first implementation of the online PlayStation Network, as well as remote connectivity between the PS3 and other Sony handheld devices. PlayStation 3, much like the Xbox 360, placed a heavy emphasis on developing online social capabilities of the console, and integrating multimedia functionality. The PS3 contains incredibly advanced hardware, just like the 360, which is very similar to that of a computer. The largest difference between the 360 and PS3, since both are extremely technologically advanced machines, is in their game content, as well as medium choice. Both consoles use optical CD drives, but the PS3 opted for Blu-ray while the 360 used HD-DVD as its high definition medium of choice. At the time of release, it was not clear which storage medium type would dominate, but this likely contributed somewhat to the future success of the PS3.

The major differences in musical content between the Xbox 360 and PS3 can be seen in their exclusive game library. While the Xbox contains more FPS, 3PS, and also racing games among their exclusive titles, the PS3 has a higher volume of exclusive action games, such as *Dante's Inferno* and the *Assassin's Creed* series. The musical requirements for action games are different than shooters, and depend on the game narrative and saturation of sound effects. There are several exclusive titles for the PS3 that have unique environments that benefit from highly individualised soundtracks. This can be observed in games such as *Assassin's Creed* (2007) in which the composer, Jesper Kyd, uses a fusion of eastern and western related instruments and musical styles to depict the setting of the crusades and the clashing/blending of two cultures and religions. One example of this includes Latin medieval-style chanting and Eastern-inspired flute solos alongside modern Western instruments. Kyd also uses non-musical sounds in the soundtrack, which increase the already diverse musical palate. In *Dante's Inferno* (2010), the music is equally evocative, with heavy string and orchestral sections, dissonant musical gestures, and most notably, string quarter tones and glissandi. Like *God of War*, the sound contains a large orchestra, choir, and heavy use of percussion. Other non-musical sounds, such as chains, serve as symbolic elements in the score, and an example of this can be seen in the listening track "Crossing the Styx". However, despite these seemingly large sounds, the music in *Assassin's Creed* and *Dante's Inferno* remains much quieter and more in the background than expected, especially during action-heavy moments, when it is dwarfed by sound effects.

Listening:

> Jesper Kyd: *Assassin's Creed*: "City of Jerusalem"
> Jesper Kyd: *Assassin's Creed*: "Acre Underworld"
> Jesper Kyd: *Assassin's Creed 2*, "Earth"
> Garry Schyman and Paul Gorman: *Dante's Inferno*,
>   "Bleeding Charon"
> Garry Schyman and Paul Gorman: *Dante's Inferno*,
>   "Crossing the Styx"
> Garry Schyman and Paul Gorman: *Dante's Inferno*,
>   "Cerberus"

5.2 Orchestral Sound

The increases in storage space, coupled with greater interest in video game music as a genre for listening outside of gameplay, contributed to the use of live orchestral recordings in certain games. This was largely dependent on a number of factors, which include both aesthetic as well as financial considerations (storage space and quality is no longer a consideration). The largest impediment to using a live orchestra is financial - a game needs a large musical budget to pay for musicians. Larger companies have more financial resources to dedicate to orchestral budgets, but this is not realistic for smaller companies. Therefore, independent games, applications, and smaller-scale releases likely do not have the budget for a full orchestra. The increased resolution and fidelity of samples has also contributed to the lack of completely orchestral recordings - composers can get orchestral-quality sound without the budget for an orchestra. Additionally, there may be times when the use of samples or synthesized sound may be an aesthetic choice, fuelled by desire for easier and more implementable interactivity, or sounds that may be unplayable by an orchestra. Nevertheless, there are many games that employ large orchestras to record the soundtrack and to achieve this desired sound.

5.2.1 Orchestra: Super Mario Galaxy (2007), Mahito Yokota and Koji Kondo

The music for *Super Mario Galaxy* was recorded using a 50-person orchestra. Originally, the music team wanted to create a soundtrack with a "Latin feel", inspired by the sounds that Kondo had used in some of the earlier games. This original sound used a lot of Latin drums and synth, but Kondo disagreed with the sound team, and eventually a soundtrack was created that included orchestral sounds, pop, and an orchestral-pop fusion.[46] It was discussed previously that the *Twilight Princess* soundtrack (another Nintendo game for Wii) did not use a live orchestra, because the team wanted a more interactive capabilities. The *Super Mario Galaxy* soundtrack used a couple of other techniques to maintain a fluid link between player action and music changes, even though the soundtrack contained live orchestral recordings. The first of these was asking the orchestra to play at different tempos, so that during gameplay, the orchestral sound would match Mario's (the player's) movements more closely.[47] The other technique that they used was to integrate the sound effects so that they blended well with the orchestral sound. The soundtrack, therefore, did not quite have the interactive freedom as a sequenced soundtrack, but the music team used creative solutions to

---

[46] "A Sound that Defines Mario." Iwata Asks, Nintendo online, http://iwataasks.nintendo.com/interviews/#/wii/super_mario_galaxy/2/1, accessed May 6, 2017.
[47] Ibid.

enhance interactivity while maintaining the musical nuance of a live recording.
Listening:

>"Overture"
>"Peach's Castle Stolen"
>"Stardust Road"

5.2.3 Sample Use: Lost Odyssey (2008), Nobuo Uematsu

Lost Odyssey was the second game scored by Nobuo Uematsu after his official departure from Square Enix (The first was *Blue Dragon,* released in 2006). The game was produced by Hironobu Sakaguchi's independent studio, Mistwalker studios. Hironobu Sakaguchi had been the producer of many of the Final Fantasy titles, and thus had a lengthy working relationship with Uematsu. The story of the game, as well as the turn-based gameplay mechanics, remained very similar to many other traditional JRPGs, and the game would not have seemed out of place as an instalment in the Final Fantasy series. These familiar mechanics ended up becoming a criticism of the game - that it lacked innovation. Nevertheless, the storyline and accompanying soundtrack was just as epic in length and scope as many other J-RPGs, and retained the quality one would expect of Nobuo Uematsu. The soundtrack primarily involved the use of orchestral samples, although certain tracks, such as "Eclipse of Time", did incorporate some live performance. The lack of orchestral use was likely due to the fact that a new, independent company, with a smaller budget, released it. Additionally, there may have been aesthetic considerations, as the types of sounds, especially in some of the battle themes, were unplayable for orchestra, and would need to be re-arranged for orchestral performance. *Lost Odyssey* also makes use of substantial post-production editing, and very refined sample control, a quality that persists throughout the HD generation and beyond.
Listening:

>"Prologue"
>"Eclipse of Time" (vocal version)
>"Epsylon Range"
>"House of the Witch"

5.3 Post-HD Games, Composers, and Listening

The consoles released after the HD generation consist of the Xbox One, PlayStation 4, and Wii U. The Wii U was released first in 2012, with the others being released in 2013. The PlayStation 4 and Xbox One both

incorporated Blu-ray players, while the Wii U maintained a proprietary optical disc format with no Blu-ray player attached. All of the systems further expanded their online services, including more downloadable content and social media applications, some of which enable users to record themselves playing and broadcast it or upload easily to social media platforms such as YouTube and Facebook. The multimedia capabilities of all systems were also expanded, a feature which is most pronounced on the Xbox One since it includes several media capabilities, including the ability to play back live television. Surround sound is also capable on all of the systems, with the Xbox One containing Dolby Digital 7.1 surround sound capabilities. Therefore, all systems of this generation are considerably advanced, and even the Wii U supports HD graphics. Nintendo also tried to modify the Wii U's controlling system to obtain a larger hardcore gaming base.
Listening:

> Wii U: David Wise: *Donkey Kong Freeze,* "Seashore War"
> Wii U: Shiho Fujii and Mahito Yokota: *New Super Mario*
>   *Bros U,* "Overworld theme"
> Inon Zur: *Fallout 4*, "Main Theme"
> Inon Zur: *Fallout 4*, "Wandering the Blasted Forest, Part I"
> Kazumi Jinnouchi: *Halo 5*, "Halo Canticles"
> Kazumi Jinnouchi: *Halo 5*, "The Trial"

5.3.1. Sound Sculpting
Game music has consistently allowed for finer degrees of control throughout history, progressing from the limitations of the NES, which prevented control devices such as volume envelopes, to the current generation, where composers and sound designers have complete freedom to sculpt sounds however they like. Many recent soundtracks feature considerable amounts of post-processing and audio effects. The examples following demonstrate the use of post-processing to sculpt sound as a means to depict a certain mood or setting. These can be extremely powerful devices, and just as the lack of envelope control led composers to avoid lengthy, exposed notes, sound sculpting encourages very subtle and detailed sounds that are very exposed. Therefore, tracks that use heavy sound sculpting techniques tend to be slower moving, and contain long held notes (or sound objects).
Listening:

> Inon Zur: *Fallout 4*, "Brightness Calling"

Ludvig Forssell: *Metal Gear Solid: The Phantom Pain*, "V Has Come To"

5.4 Online Multiplayer Games and Sound

Online gaming has made up a large share of game play prior to the HD genre, especially on PC/Mac games, but truly universal online play began with the Xbox 360 and PS3, which each had integrated live networks that were supported by nearly all of their game titles. Online functionality is now an expected component of a game, rather than a novelty, as it was on the original Xbox. It has reshaped the way people game together, bringing them out of their friends' living rooms and into a network where they can play with anyone, anywhere, and at anytime. Fully online games have their own music and sound considerations, which are dependent on the player's information load, the game setting, game genre, and lifespan of the game.

5.4.1 World of Warcraft (2005) and Online Revolution

Several online games were popular prior to the release of *World of Warcraft* in 2005, including *The Realm Online* (1996), *Meridian 59* (1995), *Everquest* (2001), and many others. However, it was *World of Warcraft* that would gain a large following, including gamers that had not played Massively Multiplayer Online games (MMOs) previously, hitting a peak number of 12 million subscribers in 2010.[48] Several *World of Warcraft* (WoW) player videos were uploaded to YouTube, including those that involved the characters performing, creating music videos, or engaging in other tasks unrelated to the gameplay. *WoW* also appeared in popular culture, including the TV show *South Park* and several advertisements. At its peak, *WoW* had such a societal impact that there were reports of employees being hired based on their *WoW* character profile and skills.[49] The popularity and prominence of *WoW* helped popularize the Massively Multiplayer Online (MMO) genre, leading to more MMO releases. This expansion continued as online capabilities for consoles improved, and as mobile devices gained the ability to run more complicated applications. While there isn't a specific type of music that is associated with online gaming, the MMO genre favours music that is not

---

[48] Purchese, Robert. "Blizzard will no longer report *World of Warcraft* subscriber numbers." Eurogamer online, Nov 4, 2011, http://www.eurogamer.net/articles/2015-11-04-blizzard-wont-report-world-of-warcraft-subscriber-numbers-anymore, accessed May 6, 2017.

[49] Pagliery, Jose. "Why I put *World of Warcraft* on my resume." CNN Money online, June 19, 2014, http://money.cnn.com/2014/06/19/technology/world-of-warcraft-resume/, accessed May 6, 2017.

overt and obtrusive, aids in setting the environment, and is sustainable for long periods of listening. This music has many of the same qualities as a previously discussed soundtrack, *Phantasy Star Online,* of the same genre. MMOs that are RPGs (MMORPGs) also contain many of the characteristics of traditional RPG soundtracks, including themes associated with characters or places.

Listening:

> Tracy Bush: *World of Warcraft*, "Legends of Azeroth"
> Tracy Bush: *World of Warcraft*, "Sacred"
> Tracy Bush: *World of Warcraft*, "Ruins"
> Nobuo Uematsu: *Final Fantasy XIV*, "Holy Consult"
> Masayoshi Soken: *Final Fantasy XIV*, "Ultima"
> Masayoshi Soken: *Final Fantasy XIV*, "Thunder Rolls"

5.5 The Rise of Mobile Games and Applications

Multi-use mobile devices have had a substantial impact on gaming in the last decade, and games for such devices have unique musical needs and challenges. The earliest mobile games appeared in the 1990s, with the most ubiquitous being *Snake*. This game was a trademark of all Nokia phones released near the turn of the millennium. The game, however, had no music, simple graphics, and very basic sound effects. The 2000s saw the rise of mobile games, first in Japan, and then in North America, especially following the release of the iPhone and other similar devices. There are a lot of reasons why such games would be appealing: the purchase of an extra (expensive) console was not required, many of the games were easy to learn and could be played for short bursts of time, and they could be played anywhere. Early smartphones had substantially less storage space than they do today, and as a result most early games for phone were simple and small in scope. The advent of the portable tablet device prompted larger-scale games to be released as applications, and as smartphones increased in storage and processing power, games designed for tablets were also released for mobile phones. Many of these games contain just as much data as CD-ROM games, and include ports of games from older consoles, including some of the Final Fantasy series. *Final Fantasy VII*, for example, was originally released on three CD-ROMs. This game has been re-released on iPhone, and can exist as a singular app stored on a phone, taking up about 2GB of storage. Mobile games have a large customer base, including people from many age ranges, and casual and hardcore gamers alike. This is due to the large variety of games that are available on smartphones, and the ubiquity of these mobile devices. The rise in mobile gaming has also had a substantial impact on consoles, since the most recent generations of consoles function as multi-use devices, and include downloadable content. Nintendo aimed to take this one step further with their most recent console, the Nintendo Switch, which was released in March 2017 and has been described as a "hybrid console" that can be used both at home and on the go as a mobile device.

5.6 Mobile Games and Apps: Composers and Listening

The library for mobile games is incredibly diverse, and the music of these games is not an exception of this diversity. Some larger-scale games contain full-length soundtracks with high quality audio, some have a few simple themes, and some consist of musical motives that are very short, ranging from 3-30 seconds. This is dependent on a range of factors, including the stylistic goals of the game, the data storage availability, the budget of the developer, and many other reasons. Unlike home consoles, users do not generally play mobile games while attached to a surround sound system, and therefore the sound tends to have less directionality than console music. The music may also serve a different function, which can be similar to that of arcade games and early NES games (to lure and engage a player), that of SNES games (to provide recognizable themes and individuality), or something else entirely.

5.6.1 Royalty-free Music

Many iOS application developers are independent, and may perhaps be limited by small budgets or small production studios. Royalty-free, or production music, presents a viable option for these games. Production music includes free and very low cost music, loops, and sound effects that developers can access without having to pay royalty fees. There are several companies and websites that provide such audio, which is generally classified by genre, mood, tempo, key, and other categories.[50] Developers can peruse these large libraries to find their desired sounds, and then either download them for free, or pay a small fee to use them. While this doesn't have the same individualistic impact as hiring a composer to write a specific score, it does allow games with lower budgets to obtain sound and music. Composers and sound designers are able to submit sounds to some of these websites and earn a small fee whenever someone downloads their works.[51] This type of music

---

[50] Stockmusic.net, audiojungle.net, freestockmusic.com, etc, there are many various sites and models.

[51] www.Rumblefish.com is an example; many of these sites do not exist anymore....

licensing is also popular in film and television, especially for low-budget independent projects that do not have the means to hire a composer.

5.6.2 Casual Games and Music

Many games for mobile devices are designed to be played in casual environments and require less continuous time commitment. While there have been some games released that are larger in scope, this has been a very recent phenomenon as data capacity on mobile devices has increased (quite drastically since about 2012). This also relates to the circumstances under which people play games on their phones as well. Much mobile gaming is done while waiting for the bus, sitting in appointment offices, or waiting for class to start, for example. Casual mobile games are intended to occupy and entertain players. This is also a goal for console games, but most console games also strive to be visually striking, and engage the player for longer uninterrupted periods. The best selling mobile games include, alongside new games, several ports of older games, including *Tetris*, *Minecraft: Pocket Edition*, and *Sonic the Hedgehog*. Currently, *Angry Birds* (2009) remains the best-selling new mobile game. Created by Rovio Entertainment, *Angry Birds* does not contain a riveting storyline, or realistic graphics, but the game has been praised for having "extremely fun physics," and being "easy to pick up and play."[52] The music, composed by Ari Pulkkinen, is equally light-hearted, upbeat, and catchy, consisting of short repetitive loops and quirky melodies. *Cut the Rope* (2010) is another very popular casual game, and the physics-based puzzle game has generated numerous sequels and spin-offs. Like *Angry Birds*, the music to *Cut the Rope* is light, catchy, and consists of short loops. There are only about two different musical loops for every Cut the Rope game - a substantial difference from console soundtracks, which can contain 100 tracks. Listening:

> Ari Pulkinnen: *Angry Birds*, "Main Theme"
> Ari Pulkinnen: *Angry Birds Rio*, "Theme"
> *Cut the Rope*, "Om Nom!"
> *Cut the Rope Experiments*, "Blueprint"

5.7 Nostalgia and Retro Gaming

Ports, re-releases, and re-masters of old games are very prevalent in the face of widespread downloadable content and HD graphics, as are new

---

[52] Podolsky, Andrew. "*Angry Birds* Review." Gamespot online, Apr 29, 2011, http://www.gamespot.com/reviews/angry-birds-review/1900-6310900/, accessed May 6, 2017.

games that have a retro feel, graphics, or sound. The decision to re-master and re-release can be made for a number of reasons: the desire to see the game as it was conceived graphically without the limitations of its time, to allow past gamers access to games for which they may no longer have consoles, to introduce a new fan base to a classic game, or general nostalgia as the generations that played these games as children are now grown up. The first reason is especially common of games like *Final Fantasy VII*, that involve long stories and cinematic sequences that are vastly improved by the processing and graphics of more powerful gaming systems, like the PS4. The surge in retro gaming is also likely an effect of the first generation of gamers reaching adulthood, and desiring the charm and simplicity of the games they played growing up, as well as current gamers seeking titles that are lighter in breadth than AAA titles, but not as simplistic as casual games. In addition to re-releases and re-masters, independent developers often choose to stylize games with a retro or historical theme, for whatever reason they see fit (aesthetics, financial, nostalgia, etc).

5.7.1 Final Fantasy Re-releases

The remaking, remixing, and re-releasing of Final Fantasy games is not an entirely novel concept; Final Fantasy games have been continuously re-released on newer game systems, ported from consoles to handheld devices, and re-mastered. However, there have been quite a few large-scale re-releases of Final Fantasy games in recent years. Both *Final Fantasy X* and *Final Fantasy VII* were re-made with High Definition sound and graphics. The *Final Fantasy VII* remake was completed in 2012 for PC, and then subsequently ported to other systems, including the PS4. The Final Fantasy X/X-2 remake was completed in 2013 for PS4. While the soundtracks of both releases remain mostly the same in terms of musical content, there is a noticeable increase in sound quality and resolution in the re-mastered versions. Additionally, games such as *Final Fantasy V-Final Fantasy IX* have all been released as iPhone apps. There is nothing remarkably different about the soundtracks, but the fact that the quantity of data, which was once an issue, can be stored on apps on a cell phone (and multiple copies at that) is notable. These type of re-releases are extensively popular as of late, and even in the cases where a re-mastering is done, the soundtracks generally retain their integrity, with improvements in fidelity and quality.

Listening (HD versions):

Masashi Hamauzu: *Final Fantasy X*, "Besaid Island"
Nobuo Uematsu: *Final Fantasy X*, "To Zanarkand"

Nobuo Uematsu and Masashi Hamauzu: *Final Fantasy X*,
   "Hymn of the Faith – Shivaz"
Nobuo Uematsu and Rikki: *Final Fantasy X*, "Suteki da ne?"
Nobuo Uematsu: *Final Fantasy VII*, "One-Winged Angel"
Nobuo Uematsu: *Final Fantasy VII*, "Aerith's Theme"

5.7.2 Shovel Knight (2014), Jake Kaufman and Manami Matsumae

The independent company Yacht Club Games developed *Shovel Knight* in 2014 after successfully using Kickstarter to crowd-fund backing. Like many other recent independently released games, the game uses retro game technology and appearance as an aesthetic choice - the game is a 2d side scrolling platform game, and uses 8-bit style graphics and sound. The gameplay and mechanics are very similar to other games of the genre, such as Mario, that were popular for the NES and SNES. The music for the game, composed by Jake Kaufman and Manami Matsumae, is consistent with 8-bit music in timbre and style, with the noise channel functioning as percussion, heavy counterpoint, and quick rhythmic action. However, while the composers try to remain within the limits of the original NES for the most part, there are some points where, for example, held notes are allowed to have a decreasing or subtly-changing volume envelope, which would not be possible on the NES.
Listening:

"Main theme"
"Steal Thy Shovel"
"One Fateful Knight"
"The Rival"

5.7.3 Minecraft (2009), Daniel Rosenfeld

Minecraft was developed by Swedish programmer Markus "Notch" Persson and released by Mojang, originally in 2009. Since then it has grown to be one of the most successful and widely distributed games, claiming 100 million users as of February 2014. The game is part of a genre called **Sandbox** games, also known as **Open World** games, in which the user is able to explore a vast world freely.[53] There are several playing modes to Minecraft now, including a survival mode and multiplayer. The game is a relatively recent release, but the graphics are reflective of nostalgic games in a unique way: the world consists of very

---

[53] "The complete history of open world games (part 2)." N4G online, http://n4g.com/news/149283/the-complete-history-of-open-world-games-part-2, accessed May 6, 2017.

pixelated graphics, but remains 3d. The music embodies this; it is ambient, repetitive, and very minimalistic at times. However, the sounds themselves are not 8- or 16-bit, and the quality is on par with current game sound. Daniel Rosenfeld, an East German composer, worked with Notch closely on the game. Rosenfeld stated that his background and situation growing up limited his formal musical education, and resulted in him learning many programs on his own. This was actually a blessing to his work on the Minecraft soundtrack, as the sound engine for the game was not very powerful, and he had to use his learned skill of producing something well with few options.[54] The soundtrack is also similar to many other Open World and online games: ambient, with slow developing processes. This is likely due to the amount of time a player will spend on the game, and the fact that the player is generally creating and exploring, rather than engaging in action and quick battles. Listening (original soundtrack):

> "Theme"
> "Subwoofer Lullaby"
> "Jukebox – Thirteen"
> "Where Are We Now?"

5.8 Outreach and Engagement

Many developments during the post-HD generation led to substantial changes in the way that composers engage with video game companies and obtain work. One of the largest changes has been the increase in use of freelance composers, as opposed to in-house musicians. There are benefits and drawbacks to freelancing, and this section explores some of the ways in which composers interact with the community in general, as well as some of the challenges (and advantages) unique to this generation.

5.8.1 Video Game and Game Music Conferences

Conferences represent an excellent opportunity for artists to meet several people at once, optimizing networking capability. Calgarian video game composer Corey de Baat, for example, stated during a lecture to a Video Game Music class that at every conference, he makes a point to distribute his contact information to at least ten people, and then to follow up with them within a week or two after the conference in order to secure the connection.[55] This can be extremely beneficial to freelancers that live

---

[54] Stuart, Keith. "How Daniel Rosenfeld wrote *Minecraft*'s music." The Guardian online, Nov 7, 2014, https://www.theguardian.com/technology/2014/nov/07/how-daniel-rosenfeld-wrote-minecraft-music, accessed May 6, 2017.

outside of major hubs such as Los Angeles, as they can make several connections at a conference and then return home. However, these conferences also result in a barrier to the economically disadvantaged, as they usually have extremely expensive registration fees, and require attendees to also cover travel costs. Registration fees for 2017 GameSoundCon in Los Angeles for example, run between 450-700 USD, and the Game Developers Conference, which takes place in San Francisco in 2017, has tickets that span from 200-2400 USD.[56] Therefore, these conferences, which are extremely vital to artist professional development, may be inaccessible to some of the composers who are most economically in need.

5.8.2 Penka Kouneva and Composer Outreach

Penka Kouneva was born in 1967 Bulgaria, and came from a very musical background, which included her composing incidental music for theatre at age twelve. She had a strong musical education, including a postgraduate education at Duke University, which resulted in her being among the first recipients of Duke's PhD in Composition.[57] Kouneva moved to Los Angeles in 1999 and composed for film for ten years, after which she began working in the video game industry. She has worked on several major titles, including *Prince of Persia: The Forgotten Sands,* and *Transformers: Revenge of the Fallen,* and has been credited both as composer and orchestrator on several such games and films. Kouneva is an active board member for GameSoundCon and has also given keynotes at conferences such as GameSoundCon to encourage young and emerging video game composers. She is a major advocate for the advancement of women composers, as well as for artist growth in general. In addition to giving keynotes on the topic, she has established Orchestral Reading sessions for Duke composers, a valuable educational opportunity for student composers. Kouneva is also active as a studio artist, and has released two award-winning concept albums, *The Woman Astronaut* (2015), and *A Warrior's Odyssey* (2012). Kouneva's assistance and encouragement is vital to the youngest generations of composers, as many composers are able to find their earliest work due to some already-established industrial connection helping them.

---

[55] Personal statement from Corey Da Baat during a guest lecture at the University of Calgary Video Game Music summer course, June 2016.

[56] See, for example, gamesoundcon.com for description of fees, accessed June 12, 2017.

[57] See Kouneva's personal website at: http://www.penkakouneva.com/, accessed June 12, 2017.

5.8.3 Issues Specific to Freelancing

Many issues also arise due to the increase in the video game composer as freelancer. In the 1980s, it was much more common for companies to have in-house sound and music teams. This has changed to a much more Hollywood-like model in which composers are contracted for specific games. Very few companies now have in-house, salaried composers. There are many benefits to this for both composers and the game companies alike. Freelancing allows composers some freedom of project choice, which results in potentially more creative freedom. The companies are also allowed to select specific composers that they feel may have a style that is suitable for the game. This will ultimately result in composers developing more of an individual voice. However, freelancing also presents many challenges, and these challenges may affect disproportionately those that are marginalized and working in less-advantaged situations (for example, working for a small independent company rather than a AAA company). Depending on the location you are working in, there are little protections afforded to freelancers regarding payment, non-payment, and receipt of money. Only very recently has the state of New York, for example, put protections in place ensuring that freelancers received proper payment within 30 days of project completion.[58] Additionally, freelancing may or may not allow for the composer to receive benefits such as health insurance, depending on their personal situation. This also varies based on location and results in some freelancers being afforded certain privileges that others or not. For example, a freelancer in Canada will receive basic provincial healthcare regardless of hours worked or income level, but this may not be the case in some places in the US. Finally, freelancing doesn't allow for secure continuous income, which also benefits the already privileged, who may have savings and family safety nets that can help them to stick it out through the hard times. Those in economically disadvantaged situations will find themselves potentially unable to survive a lengthy break in paid contracts, resulting in the need for other employment, which will then result in less time to network and get new contracts. Freelancers may also have a more difficult time than salaried composers obtaining long-term loans such as mortgages.

---

[58] Whitford, Emma. "NYC's 'Freelance Isn't Free' Act Goes Into Effect Today." Gothamist Online, May 15, 2017, http://gothamist.com/2017/05/15/freelancer_law_nyc.php, accessed June 12, 2017.

5.9 The Future of Game Sound

Game sound evolved considerably following the release of HD consoles, although these developments are not timbral liberations like occurred in the 16-bit generation, or liberations in scope/length such as those that occurred in the 32-bit generation. A large development during this generation has been the use of space. This includes space in frequency, the spatialization and spatial placement between the musical sound and the sound effects, and the interactive spatialization of sounds in gameplay. This parallels the graphic development of the time, as games became more realistically 3D, with clearer resolution, and therefore clearer visual object separation. The move towards more immersive sound has advanced quite a bit during this generation, with implementations using Dolby 7.1 surround sound. VR systems have been released for personal use within the last year, including a system released especially for the PS4. Whether these VR hardware options will end up becoming ubiquitous in console gaming is still unknown (it is currently expensive and requires the user to wear something on their head), however, the impact it will have on game sound is likely to be huge, even if this technology does not gain widespread use. Holographic images, and other 3D images may also find eventual integration in gameplay. As immersive technology expands, players have to keep track of a lot more at any given time during gameplay, and immersive, 3D sound aids in providing additional cues to the user. This enhanced feedback has been extended to controllers as well, which provide more haptic feedback during gameplay (and in the case of the WiiMotes, aural feedback as well). Gaming requires the player to engage with several senses at the same time, and involves perceiving aural, visual, and haptic cues. This means that gaming is essentially a multimodal experience, and the sound and music should reflect this. At the same time, alongside all of the increases in technology and resolution in AAA titles, there is an expansion within retro and casual gaming community. Apps, downloadable arcade games, and remakes are popular with casual gamers that are seeking games that can be played without large time commitments. This also may be due to the generation of gamers that played Nintendo as children becoming adults, and seeking some of the nostalgia and charm of the early systems. For new gamers, these retro and nostalgic games can seem exotic and new, and perhaps an alternative to expensive and time-consuming large-scale games. Therefore, the current generation of games is an incredibly diverse one. With so much game diversity, there is diversity in game sound and music. Composers also have a wider variety of companies to choose from, including independent companies and large AAA companies.

5.9.1 Working for Independent Game Companies

Recently there have also been several independent game composers that have gained mainstream acknowledgement and success, without scoring for AAA companies. The change in game distribution as well as the general online accessibility of games and of knowledge has contributed to this phenomenon – prior to these changes it would have been extremely difficult for independent games themselves to receive mainstream acknowledgement, let alone individual composers.

Danny Baronowsky (b. 1984)

Danny Baronowsky represents a modern tale of success, both in his ability to gain traction as a freelance composer, and in his ability to distribute his music over the internet. Baronowsky attempted to make a living as a freelance film composer for seven years, but this career never took off – there simply isn't the money in film that there used to be, the market is over-saturated, and Baronowsky claimed to have made a total of 2000 in his entire 7 year attempt.[59] He was, however, successful in game music, finding many jobs and higher price points working for independent game companies. He composed the music to the independent hit *Super Meat Boy* (2010), which helped him establish a name for himself as a composer. Another soundtrack he has composed the music for is *Crypt of the Necrodancer* (2015), which contains a musical component within the gameplay- characters can only attack on the beat of the music. Currently, he is also signed to write the music for Minecraft creator "Notch"'s next game. Baronowsky stated no desire to join a AAA company, explaining that, "I think it would be less money, and less fun, and I wouldn't have the rights to my music."[60] Retaining the rights to his music enables him to make more income, as he can then sell his music online himself. Working for independent companies also allows him more flexibility regarding residence, and unlike many of his AAA-employed counterparts, he lives in Phoenix, AZ, rather than Los Angeles.

Jessica Curry (b. 1973)

Jessica Curry was born in Liverpool, and has a postgraduate degree in film music from the National Film and Television School. She helped to co-found, along with her husband, the video game company The Chinese

---

[59] Hamilton, Kirk. "Video Games are the New Best Way to Make a Living Composing Music." Kotaku Online, Feb 23, 2012, http://kotaku.com/5887745/video-games-are-the-new-best-way-to-make-a-living-composing-music, accessed June 12, 2017.
[60] Ibid.

Room. Following several successful releases, such as *Dear Esther* and *Amnesia: A Machine for Pigs,* The Chinese Room developed a Sony exclusive title, *Everybody's Gone to the Rapture.* The game, released in 2015, would eventually lead her to win a BAFTA award for the music in 2016.[61] However, working under the new conditions (for a mainstream publisher, Sony) also resulted in her departing from the Chinese Room, citing issues with her degenerative disease, issues with the commercial company, and gender-related mistreatment.[62] This indicates that there are many advantages to remaining independent, despite the financial benefits that commercial success can bring.

5.9.2 Working for AAA Companies

Jeremy Levy was featured in the same publication as Danny Baronowsky, representing a contrasting example of a composer working for a AAA company. Unlike Baronowsky, Levy lives and works in Los Angeles, because this is much more important for those working in AAA games that may need to be consistently present (and on- site). Additionally, Levy takes on several jobs outside of composition, including working as a session trombonist, an orchestrator, and an arranger. Levy says he has done every sort of "grunt" work, including orchestration, sitting as a session musician, and "anything he can get his hands on"[63] He did orchestration for several video games, including *Batman: Arkham City, Infamous 2, God of War III,* as well as many TV shows. Like Baronowsky (and many others working in video game music), Levy had to network to get himself established. He had connections from both touring as a musician, and as a student at UMiami. When he moved to Hollywood he got a list of contacts from one of his old professors, and managed to obtain work through these contacts.[64] For the most part, his job is very different from that of an independent composer; he doesn't have the same locational freedom, and he won't retain the rights to most of his compositions. This also means that he has some protection through the California Musician's Union,

---

[61] See full list of winners at: http://awards.bafta.org/award/2016/games?, accessed June 12, 2017.

[62] See Curry's post on the Chinese Room Blog from October 9, 2015 at: http://www.thechineseroom.co.uk/blog/blog/why-im-sort-of-leaving-the-chinese-room, accessed June 12, 2017.

[63] Hamilton, Kirk. "Video Games are the New Best Way to Make a Living Composing Music." Kotaku Online, Feb 23, 2012, http://kotaku.com/5887745/video-games-are-the-new-best-way-to-make-a-living-composing-music, accessed June 12, 2017.

[64] Ibid.

however. While Levy stated that he likes his work, he also stated that he is unsure of the sustainability of the work, and that it tends to fall upon the whims of what the AAA companies want at any given moment. Currently, music and sound are highly valued components of games (and are practically an industry in and of themselves) and therefore composers are in great demand, but especially as algorithmic composition becomes more efficient, it is unclear what will transpire in the future.

5.10 Conclusion

When studying classical musical history, it is common to trace threads between social and political acts and the changing climate of the music. Historical events affect music for a multitude of reasons, including cultural taste, political use of the arts, championing certain themes associated with political platforms, and the surplus or lack of funds. Video game music faces a similar relationship with the development of technology, as well as consumer patterns. This can be seen in the earlier generations, as more advanced systems produced sound cards capable of producing more diverse sounds. Once streaming audio was implemented, sound advances were primarily made in quality, with larger advances made in style and diversity, as games followed suit, ranging in genre from hardcore hack and slash games, to small-scale casual apps. Overall, we can see that, over time, timbral diversity increased, control over sound increased, and individuality became important to game music. In the post-HD (current) era, excellent sound and graphics are no longer a novelty, and gamers are seeking to play nostalgic games as well. Social media/internet sharing and media dissemination is a huge advancement that has contributed to more independent developers making games, some of which are nostalgic. Possibilities of this generation are numerous, since consumers have more choice and developers have more options for producing and distributing their media. Therefore, the future trajectory video game music remains as uncertain as to which next-generation console will end up dominating. However, we can predict that new technologies such as VR will likely have a large impact, as well as the general increased interest in game music (and especially classic game music) and immersive sound.

SECTION II: THE THEORY OF VIDEO GAME MUSIC

Chapter 6: Terminology and Concepts in Music for Interactive Media

This chapter explores some of the terminology relating to music, which is also applicable to sound effects, for interactive media. We will explore degrees with which music is interactive within games, as well as some of the methods that are used to create sound that can repeat indefinitely. These two concepts, interactivity and continuous sound, are specific to music for interactive media; music for film does not contain these qualities because movies are a permanent, fixed, and a linear medium, and therefore the sound will always be fixed the same way to the picture. It is possible that this may evolve and change in the future, but unlikely unless films become interactive media themselves. In addition to interactive-media specific terminology, we do explore some concepts that relate to film music theory in this chapter as well that are also applicable to games.

By the end of this chapter, you should be able to:

1) Label a piece of music (with justification for such labels) using the terminology discussed,
2) Understand some of the challenges of creating music for essentially unending media, and
3) Describe some of the techniques used by composers of interactive and unending media.

6.1 What is Interactive?

It is easy to assume that since video games are by nature interactive, that all music for games is inherently "interactive music". However, this is not necessarily the case. Theories on what interactive music precisely means are plentiful, and a consensus on the matter has only been tentatively reached. We can look to discussion surrounding interactivity in concert music for some parallels: Jon Drummond states in "Understanding Interactive Systems" with regards to interactive concert music technology, that, "the description of interactive in these instances is often a catchall term that simply implies some sense of audience control or participation in an essentially reactive system."[65] This is primarily due to the large quantity of works for, for example, live instrument and electronics being termed "interactive", when the instrument is merely being amplified and processed during performance of a notated score. This in itself does not produce any interactivity

---

[65] Drummond, Jon. "Understanding interactive systems." Organised Sound 14.02 (2009): 124-133.

between the performer and the electronics; the performer executes a score, and the electronics react in whatever way they are programmed to do so. Robert Rowe, in his 1991 publication *Interactive Music Systems*, proposes the following definition of interactive music, which does not exclude the performance situation described above: "Interactive computer music systems are those whose behaviour changes in response to musical input. Such responsiveness allows these systems to participate in live performances, of both notated and improvised music."[66] This definition, however, also does not address the fact that interaction should involve responsiveness on part of the performer as a result of the electronic sound, as well. The study of game music is younger than the study of concert electroacoustic and electronic music, so theories regarding interactivity of music in games are fewer. However, the usual definition of interactive music in games is closer to Rowe's, disregarding Drummond's concern that it may be reactive instead. Therefore, game music has been accepted generally as interactive music, but there remains significantly less discourse surrounding the nature of interactivity in game sound. In the approach taken in this text, I expand upon Rowe's definition, which applies to electronic concert music, and suggest that for game music to be truly interactive, the music's behaviour must change actively in response to an intentional **musical** input by the player. Additionally, true interactivity of music should be a two-way exchange between the "performer" and the technology. This distinction is more difficult in media such as video games because the exchange between player and technology is not always obvious or intentional. I may enter a dungeon, and as a result the music changes to be ominous, and so I decide to back out of the dungeon accordingly. This is somewhat of an interactive exchange, but at the same time, I am not engaging with the game to intentionally change the music; I am engaging with the game and the music changes as an inherent result. Therefore, I also suggest that music for games is an interactive media that exists on a continuum, containing varying degrees of interactivity: **reactive, adaptive,** and **fully interactive.** I will describe each in detail below, including examples.

6.2 Reactive Music

A quote earlier by Drummond stated that most music we consider interactive in the concert hall is essentially reactive. This is due to some works, containing live electronics, claiming themselves to be interactive, or "with interactive electronics", without careful consideration of the

---

[66] Rowe, Robert. *Interactive music systems: machine listening and composing.* MIT press, 1992.

implications of the term **interactive**. A work for flute and electronic processing, for example, may not require any response on part of the player to the electronic sound, and merely require that the flautist plays written notes, and the electronics process this music according to prewritten algorithms. There is no interaction here, and it could therefore be termed reactive: the performer plays, the music responds, and the performer continues to play, without adjusting to the electronic effects or responding in kind. An extension of this can be applied to video game music. The term **reactive** refers to music that changes in response to a singular non-musical action of the player. An example of such music would be when Mario goes down a pipe, and the music changes from overworld to underworld music. Another example would be in early *Final Fantasy* games, when the music cuts from dungeon music to battle music when a random encounter begins. Both of these situations involve the character executing an action, and the music **reacting** to the player's action, with a singular musical response. There are two important distinctions to make regarding reactive music that separate it from adaptive and fully interactive music. Reactive music is not fully interactive, because the player does not actively participate in modifying the music - rather, the music changes as a result of an unrelated, non-musical action. It is not adaptive because it does not continuously update and modify itself. There is a singular action that has a singular result, and this result remains until another modifying action is made by the player. Reactive music is less common in modern video games than in games of the PlayStation era and before because there are more opportunities for creating smooth musical response within adaptive music. However, there are situations in which composers may seek reactive music for aesthetic reasons.

6.2.1 Reactive Music Examples
Reactive music was widespread during the 8-bit and 16-bit generations of all consoles, and persisted through 32-bit systems. It is a less common form of interactive music today, but still exists in certain game genres. Of all the types of interactivity, reactive music may seem to be the simplest, and this may be a correct interpretation. However, the concept and origins of reactive music indicate that it is innovative, and sets a precedent for adaptive music. It is also important to consider the music as a function of the environment; currently games involve fully immersive, 3d worlds that a player can seamlessly explore, often without fade screens. This was not the case in 8-bit through 32-bit consoles, where continuous motion occurred on a 2-dimensional plane, or players explored a pseudo-3D space, and upon reaching the end of a screen, the

screen would fade to the next screen. This fading is a visual analogue to reactive sound, as music fades out and then fades back in. Examples of this are easily noticed in games such as *Final Fantasy*, where a player reaches the end of a location, the screen fades out, the music fades out, and then a new screen and music fade in. Another very clear example occurs in the original *Super Mario Bros.* game, when Mario has to go down a pipe into the underworld. In this case, rather than combining a fade of audio and visuals, the overworld music cuts out abruptly as Mario slides down the pipe, during which time a pipe sound effect plays, and as soon as Mario emerges from the pipe, the underworld music begins. Both the fade and the sound effect/action separation are means with which music changes reactively, but incorporates a smooth transition.

6.3 Adaptive Music

Adaptive music is probably the most commonly integrated type of interactive music discussed in this text, steadily increasing in its use since the late 1990s. Adaptive music involves continuous modification of music based on player's actions, but without the intentional and active correlation between player action and sound. Much like reactive music, the changes that occur in adaptive music happen as a result of non-musical player actions. However, unlike reactive music, this process is more continuous. A definition of adaptive music, taken from the Electroacoustic Resource Site (EARS), states:

> The non-linear medium of computer gaming can lead a player down an enormous number of pathways to an enormous number of resolutions. From the standpoint of music composition, this means that a single piece may resolve in one of an enormous number of ways. Event-driven music engines (or adaptive audio engines) allow music to change along with game state changes. Event-driven music isn't composed for linear playback; instead, it's written in such a way as to allow a certain music sequence (ranging in size from one note to several minutes of music) to transition into one or more other music sequences at any point in time.[67]

Adaptive music has been steadily replacing reactive music in contemporary games because sound engines are more flexible and allow for more incremental changes in music. Adaptive music is also the most diverse; the adaptation can be as subtle as instruments dropping in and

---

[67] EARS ElectroAcoustic Resource Site, "Definition of Adaptive Sound." http://ears.pierrecouprie.fr/spip.php?article17, Accessed May 21, 2016.

out of the mix or the overall volume decreasing slightly, or can involve the entire soundtrack continuously changing from note to note, depending on actions taken by the player.

6.3.1 Adaptive Precedents: Monkey Island 2: LeChuck's Revenge (1991)

The intention behind the term adaptive is derived due to the process with which the music is affected during gameplay, rather than simply the result. This process originated with the creation of the sound engine iMUSE, developed by Michael Land and Peter McConnell at LucasArts in the early 1990s.[68] This engine improved the interactive capabilities of sound by changing the way that sound is modified during the game. The designers desired the ability to change music fluidly throughout the game, in contrast to the abrupt changes that occur during reactive sound transitions. The iMUSE system was a forerunner in the revolutionizing of game sound, and would leave a lasting impression on the interactivity of game sound. iMUSE uses several techniques to allow for the music to adapt organically to gameplay. One of the ways that iMUSE enables smooth transitions is the playing back of smaller portions of loops at certain points while waiting to check if certain gaming conditions are met.[69] Since early computers had variances in processing power, a cut scene would take longer on one computer than another. This waiting process enabled the music to remain consistent during the cut scene, and adapt to the processing speed of the computer. Another example is demonstrated in *Monkey Island 2: LeChuck's Revenge*: when the main character wanders around and different variations of the main theme play, with different instrumentations.[70] This is a precedent of a technique, called vertical re-orchestration, which will be discussed in detail later in the chapter.

6.3.2 Vertical Re-orchestration and Horizontal Re-sequencing

Two techniques that are commonly associated with adaptive music are vertical re-orchestration and horizontal re-sequencing. **Horizontal re-sequencing** involves the breaking down of a musical composition into several smaller sequences or segments that can be re-arranged to create

---

[68] Collins, Karen. *Game Sound*, p. 51

[69] Mackey, Bob, "Day of the Tentacle Composer Peter McConnell on Communicating Cartoniness." US Gamer online, Mar 7, 2016, http://www.usgamer.net/articles/day-of-the-tentacle-composer-peter-mcconnell-on-communicating-cartooniness, accessed May 6, 2017.

[70] Mackey, Bob. "iMUSE and the Secret of Organic Music." 1UP online (archived), June 2012, http://archive.is/ZDzV9, accessed May 6, 2017.

variant copies of the same work. In *A Composer's Guide to Game Music,* Winifred Phillips describes horizontal re-sequencing as an analogue to Mozart's musical dice game:

> In the musical dice game attributed to Mozart, musical pieces are broken down into segments consisting of the contents of a single measure. These segments are assigned numbers. Rolling the dice results in numbers that are used to determine which of these musical segments comes next in the resulting composition. Mozart composed the segments so that they could be juggled and recombined in nearly endless combinations. His game is, in fact, a low-tech but mathematically complex demonstration of a *horizontal re-sequencing* method.[71]

This process described above is similar to those taken during horizontal re-sequencing, as algorithms within the game's programming decide what order the segments are played in. Instead of rolling dice as in the example above, however, the choices are determined by computer code in the game. There are several ways to approach segment selection, including random selection, selection by probability, selection from a specific set of audio files at a specific time, and many more. The end result is a soundtrack that is continuous, but never repetitive. The composer must keep in mind when writing the music what the combination possibilities are, and compose music/create sounds that are acceptable when combined in many ways. As a result, music that uses horizontal re-sequencing may not always have the individual, distinct voice that through-composed music does. However, discussions on aesthetics of horizontally re-sequenced music, as it becomes more common, may lead to new compositional developments and techniques.

Vertical re-orchestration, which is also sometimes referred to as *vertical layering,* or *interactive stems,* involves the breaking down of a musical composition into several smaller components that can be layered on top of one another simultaneously to form different orchestrations of the same composition. Vertical re-orchestration is essentially very similar to horizontal re-sequencing, except that rather than sections of music being re-arranged in time, sections of music are re-arranged vertically by changing the instrumentation. The technique can be used to great effect, especially in situations where a short loop is played over and over. The continuously changing instrumentation gives the loop a dynamism it

---

[71] Phillips, Winifred, *A Composer's Guide to Game Music*, MIT Press, 2014.

wouldn't have otherwise. Vertical re-orchestration is therefore an excellent approach for creating dynamic loops, which will be discussed later in the chapter.

6.3.3 Other Adaptive Musical Changes: Tempo and Volume

Changes in tempo and volume are also used in adaptive game music. A very early example of this is in the game *Space Invaders* (1978): the music speeds up when the player is getting close to failure, and slows down as the player begins to succeed at the game. Such changes can be very valuable to gameplay, giving gameplay feedback to the player that is related to the current conditions in the game (e.g., player succeeding, player failing, player about to die). This type of adaptive music tends to be more perceptibly linked to the game, as re-sequencing and re-orchestration are often either random techniques (even though they may have their own hierarchical decision making models), or they are more linked to game actions that have little to do with the soundtrack music. Another example of music speeding up is in the game *Tetris* (1984): as soon as the blocks reach a certain height, music will play back extremely fast to signify that the player is about to lose, and then slows once the player has cleared enough blocks to be safe again. However, unlike in *Space Invaders*, the *Tetris* music only speeds up once the blocks have reached a certain point, remains at that speed, and then slows down once the blocks are below that point. Therefore, in *Tetris*, these speed changes are actually somewhat reactive. Volume changes are also a common element of adaptive game music. Music may fade out when sound effects play, for example, or when the user walks away from or towards a certain area. In the game *Bioshock* (2007), as the player nears certain objects such as radios that are playing music, their volume increases. Volume and tempo changes do not create as apparent of a change to the music as vertical re-orchestration and horizontal re-sequencing, but they can give valuable aural feedback to the player.

6.3.4 Algorithmically Adaptive Music

Algorithmically adaptive music includes soundtracks in which a majority of the music is generated by algorithms as a result of gameplay. While this may sound a lot like fully interactive music, it is different because the player generates the music passively; there is no active participation in the musical creation. One of the most overt examples of this type of music is in the game *Rez* (2001), released for the PlayStation 2. *Rez* is a sci-fi based shooter, in which the player's movements and actions determine every component of the soundtrack. All of the sound effects are replaced with synthesized musical sounds, and the movements of the player determine the speed of an electronic beat.[72] The result is a soundtrack that is very connected to player performance, but the lack of sound effects, especially because they blend in with the music, can be quite disorienting to those accustomed to shooters that have a large separation between sound effects and music. Nevertheless, the concept is intriguing, and results in unique gameplay. Another example of algorithmically adaptive music is presented in the game *Red Dead Redemption,* released in 2010. This game involves the use of several different pre-recorded stems, which are then combined and played back based on algorithms that select those stems depending on certain game parameters.[73] The connection between the sound and the gameplay is significantly looser, but it provides a soundtrack that is dynamic and does not get repetitive. The soundtrack is also different every time the game is played. This technique represents a type of horizontal re-sequencing, although it is not considered looping due to the continuously generated nature of the soundtrack. While horizontal re-sequencing contains small audio components that can be re-arranged to create individual pieces within the game, every audio stem in *Red Dead Redemption* can be combined with any other audio stem in any order.

6.4 Fully Interactive Music

Fully interactive music, as defined by this text, is only possible when a player performs an action within a game intended to have a direct impact on the music. This process does involve a two-way exchange between the player and the music: the player performs an action that actively results in a sound, listens for the result, and performs the subsequent action accordingly. Fully interactive music is present in its most obvious form in music games like *Rock Band* or *Guitar Hero*, but also exists in areas within games, in mini-games, and when musical actions are a component of the game.

6.4.1 Music-based Games

Music-based video games enjoyed their peak during the late 2000s, following a rise in popularity of the game *Guitar Hero*, originally released in 2005, and its subsequent competitor, the multiplayer game *Rock Band* (2007). Karaoke games also saw popularity during this time.

---

[72] Parkin, Simon. "Oral history of *Rez* recounts a marriage of game and music." Gamasutra online, March 17, 2016, http://www.gamasutra.com/view/news/268364/Oral_history_of_Rez_recounts_a_ma rriage_of_game_and_music.php, accessed May 6, 2017.

[73] See video online at: http://www.rockstargames.com/newswire/article/7361/behind-the-scenes-of-the-red-dead-redemption-soundtrack.html, accessed May 6, 2017.

Donkey Konga, a music-based game starring familiar Nintendo Characters Donkey and Diddy Kong, preceded the *Guitar Hero* and *Rock Band* series, appearing on GameCube in 2003. In *Donkey Konga,* the player uses peripheral conga controllers to play along with on screen instructions; these instructions are then presented in a scrolling tablature that instructs the player to either hit the conga or clap. This type of scrolling tablature would persist through later music-based games such as *Guitar Hero. Guitar Hero* popularized the music-based game genre, eventually becoming one of the best-selling games for the PS2, despite the high retail price of the guitar controller required for gameplay.[74] *Rock Band* was released following the unexpected success of *Guitar Hero*, and featured a full band set-up, including vocals, drums, guitar, and bass. The *Rock Band* instrumental kit retailed at nearly 250 USD upon its release, but it would still proceed to be a popular game, and inspired *Guitar Hero* to release a full band equivalent as well. Sequels for both have been continuously released (the most recent *Rock Band* iteration hit shelves in late 2015). However, the popularity has waned slightly over time, likely due to the expensive peripherals, other musical party games, such as *Dance Central*, being released, and a general decline in interest in party games. Nevertheless, these music-based games continue to be produced and released to good reception, indicating that music-based games provide a solid platform for gameplay.

6.4.2 In-game Activities

Sometimes interactive music does not exist as part of the overall gameplay, but within small mini-games, or tasks the player has to complete during the game. An extended example of this would be in *Ocarina of Time* or *Wind Waker*, in which the player has to press certain buttons to play certain learned melodies (as in *Ocarina of Time*), or conduct (as in *Wind Waker*). These tasks create fully interactive music because the user is actively engaging with the sound to achieve a desired musical result. These results also happen to have an impact on the gameplay. In both Zelda games, for example, they are integral components to the storyline and advancement. Sometimes in-game interactive music does not have an effect on the overall gameplay, such as in *Grand Theft Auto*. In *GTA*, players will hear a radio when they are in a car, and they have the option to change the station, or turn the radio off entirely. Again, this is an instance in which the player intentionally changes a musical component of the game, rendering it fully interactive.

---

[74] Zezima, Katie. "Virtual Frets, Actual Sweat." NY Times online, July 15, 2007, http://www.nytimes.com/2007/07/15/fashion/15guitar.html, accessed May 6, 2017.

This element of *GTA* is one of the components that give the game the open world, sandbox setting. Interactive in-game music is also present in another sandbox game, *Minecraft*, as the player can change what music they play on a jukebox. These in-game musical activities can also present as very small mini-games or components on larger quests, such as in *Eternal Sonata* (2007), when Allegro and his team have to replicate a Chopin melody on a large floor piano in order to proceed. In-game interactive music, therefore, can have a large-scale impact on the game, or no real impact on gameplay at all, but it always gives the player a feeling of more control over the musical environment of the game.

6.4.3 Music as Primary Game Component: Sound Shapes (2012), Various Composers

Sound Shapes (2012), developed by Queasy studios in Toronto, is a side-scrolling game in which the creation of music becomes a primary component of the game.[75] The game follows the player, who is represented by a ball on the screen, as they proceed through the adventure, avoiding obstacles and attempting to collect notes. Collecting notes results in the build-up of the music during gameplay. There are two effects that result when a player collects a note: first, the player receives immediate pitched musical feedback that a note has been collected, and this is followed by an increase in the musical density as a layer is added to the soundscape. Essentially, proceeding through the levels creates a song. There is also a gameplay type called creation mode, similar to a looping sequencer, in which the player places notes on a screen as a scroll bar continuously loops through the sequence. This enables the player to create their own levels and shapes, and essentially, their own music. While some of the elements may not seem to be precisely one-to-one correlated as in the other fully interactive music we have discussed, this game involves an intentional player-driven musical result. The music is the object of the gameplay, not a passive result of gameplay that has other, non-musical goals. Therefore, for the purposes of the classification in this text, we will refer to a game such as *Sound Shapes* as having fully interactive sound.

6.5 Not All Music

As you play through games on your own, you may realize that not all of the music in games fits nicely into these categories. *Sound Shapes*, for example, is described here as interactive, but upon examining the background music only, one could also make a case for it being adaptive.

---

[75] *Sound Shapes*, Sony Computer Entertainment, 2013.

Especially as the possibilities in games increases, music in games will continuously evolve. However, the important message to take away from this is that we cannot group all video game music together as interactive simply because gameplay is interactive, and, if we are to properly study video game music, we must assess it as its own entity rather than an extension of gameplay. It also brings to the forefront the importance of music in games, either as a passive reactor of player actions that enhances player responsiveness, or as a component of the gameplay. Unlike films, video games include interactive involvement on part of the player, and feedback is essential to situations containing human-computer interaction. Sound is just one of the feedback systems that games use (in addition to visual and now, haptic feedback), and it is therefore important to evaluate the function of the sound within the player experience.

6.6 Unending Music

One of the elements of gameplay that sets it apart from film is that it is not a linear media that will exist for the same duration with the same events every time it is played. It is not even possible to determine the length of specific levels and areas within a game, because every player will spend a different time at each task. Therefore, composers and sound designers must create a music that can be played indefinitely during gameplay. The easiest way to do this is to have music that loops repeatedly so long as some condition is met during the game (i.e., you are in a specific area). **Looping** music became a standard for video game music, although other types of music would emerge, such as **linear** music, in response to FMVs, and **generative** music, which became possible as sound engines became more advanced and allowed music to be generated in real time. We will examine in this section how the loop has evolved, especially with regards to the ways that sound teams implement variations in loops to make the music sound similar but not tedious. We will also examine the involvement of linear and generative music, and examples of the use of both within games.

6.7 Looping Music

Looped music exists dating as far back as some of the early arcade games, with *Rally-X* (1980) being the first example of a truly musical looping soundtrack (*Space Invaders* had a continuous background soundtrack that looped, but it consisted of only four notes repeated over and over). Loops were originally static, unchanging, and very short, due to space, processing, and programming restrictions. Looping length and dynamism increased over time, giving rise to the extended linear loop, and dynamic loops that are continuously changing.

6.7.1 Linear Loops

The majority of early looping music is linear; the loop progresses, and once it reaches a certain point, the loop simply repeats, exactly the way it was played the first time. Linear loops do not change based on the gameplay, unless the gameplay directs the music to change to a different linear loop. Composers sought some diversity within linear loops, so that they wouldn't get boring, but they do repeat endlessly, without variation. An example of a linear looping piece of music is the Mario Overworld theme. Every time it is completed, it repeats, exactly as it was stated before. However, Koji Kondo creates some variation within this loop by structuring it in a less predictable way: he reorders smaller segments of the composition so that the themes are not always played in the same order. This resulting pattern is not simply a repeating back and forth of two or three different themes, and the adjustments to the order of the sections suggests that keeping the loop interesting was a concern for the composer. During the 16-bit and 32-bit eras, it was possible to make longer linear loops, which allowed for more variance. However, these loops would still repeat endlessly, over and over. And while this may be the desire of a composer, especially in situations where character or location themes are at the forefront of the compositional intention, rather than interactivity, sound teams increasingly sought ways to vary these loops and add dynamism to the music.

6.7.2 Dynamic Loops

It is also possible to have music that loops or repeats itself in the game with minor variations. One example of such variation would be in a piece of music that is both looping and uses vertical re-orchestration. While the loop is occurring continuously, the instruments change, making the loop dynamic. This method of looping is very common in games with very short loops, especially mobile games and casual games. Transposition can also be used to change loops; an early example of using transposition to add dynamism to a loop is in the game *Rally-X*, as the 2-bar theme is transposed to a lower pitch the second time. The soundtrack for *Rally-X* itself, however, is not a dynamic loop. In order for such a technique to be dynamic, the transposition would have to happen differently each time the loop occurs, or at least during some of the times the loop occurs. This is possible currently, and adding a slight adjustment such as a transposition during loops can be subtle but effective. The general intent behind dynamic loops is that the music is allowed to remain the same, but not become tedious. Martin O'Donnell stated, regarding the *Halo* soundtrack, that:

> The most important feature... is that it contains enough permutations and the proper randomization so that players do not feel like they're hearing the same thing repeated over and over. Even the greatest and most satisfying sound, dialog or music will be diminished with too much repetition. It is also important to have the ability to randomize the interval of any repetition. It might be difficult to get the sound of one crow caw to be vastly different from another, but the biggest tip off to the listener that something is artificial is when the crow always caws after the leaf rustle and before the frog croak every thirty seconds or so. The exception to that rule are specific game play sounds that need to give the player immediate and unequivocal information, such as a health meter.[76]

6.8 Linear Music

Not all situations in games are nonlinear, and therefore not all music is required to loop. Especially with the rise of FMVs, linear music is needed at certain times in games. FMV cut scenes that break out of gameplay mode generally use linear music. Title sequences can be another example of linear music. While the title music does loop, the video loops along with it, creating a picture lock. The difference between this and looping music is the function and compositional intent; rather than the experience of interactive gameplay and music that will match the visuals differently as it loops, the music and the picture are always the same, and it is essentially as if you are replaying the same movie over and over. The exception to this is title sequences in which the screen locks on the menu select once the sequence is finished, but for the purposes of this book, I will still term this music linear because of its function and intent. Another important clarification to make regarding linear music is that it is not the same as linear looped music. While the two terms do sound very similar, looping linear music is designed to accompany gameplay, creating a never-ending musical background to ever-changing visuals. As the need for FMVs to cut away from gameplay decreases due to higher processing power in consoles, linear music within the game (away from the title sequence) becomes less common.

---

[76] Collins, Karen, *Playing With Sound: A Theory of Interacting With Sound and Music in Video Games*, MIT press, 2013.

6.9 Generative Music

Generative music includes any type of music that is generated in game, based on pre-written algorithms that determine what musical sounds to play next. An example of generative music that we already examined above would (loosely) be the game *Rez,* where the player generates a soundtrack during gameplay. Another example of generative music is the game *Spore* (2008), an online game that uses the interactive music software Pure Data (PD) to generate the score based on pre-written algorithms. The game follows the player as they develop a species from the very beginnings of single-celled life through complex civilization. This method of gameplay is essentially generative, with the results of the development dependent on player actions and pre-written game algorithms. Therefore, generative music presents an appropriate backdrop to the gameplay, as the music is generated based on the actions of the game, which are generated by the actions of the player. While generative music can sound a lot like dynamic looping, the difference between the two is that generative music progresses endlessly, with no components that behave in a looping manner. Horizontal re-sequencing can be an element used in a type of generative music, but horizontal re-sequencing is conceptually a type of dynamic looping music. However, there are situations in which a large number of pre-recorded stems are played back throughout the game based on a pre-designed algorithm in which these stems are not part of a specific composition in the game. An example of this is *Red Dead Redemption*, which consists of a multitude of stems, recorded by the music team, which are selected for playback throughout the game algorithmically. In order to make it possible for any of the stems to accompany any others, the musicians intentionally recorded all of the stems in the same key.[77] When evaluating the music based solely on this concept, one could evaluate the soundtrack as one singular large dynamic loop. However, the composers created the stems with the knowledge that there would be several different tracks within the game. Therefore, just as in the distinctions between interactive/reactive/adaptive music, the distinction between generative music and dynamic looping music lies in the musical intention: one is designed to provide variance to looping music, the other is designed to create music that is continuously new.

---

[77] Stuart, Keith, "Redemption Songs: the Making of the *Red Dead Redemption* Soundtrack." The Guardian online, May 26, 2010, https://www.theguardian.com/technology/gamesblog/2010/may/26/red-dead-redemption-soundtrack, accessed May 6, 2017.

6.10 Character Perception of Music

For the most part in games, soundtracks exist outside of the world that the character is experiencing. However, there is sometimes music and/or sound that a character in the game can hear. These types of player-experienced sounds are called **diegetic** sounds, whereas soundtrack elements that a player cannot hear within the game are called **non-diegetic.**[78] These terms are derived from film music theory, but are applicable to game music as well. Non-diegetic music in video games generally consists of soundtrack elements, although some soundtrack elements (such as a radio playing) may be diegetic. Diegetic music is present in many games, consisting of music that the player may create, as well as music that is heard within the environment. This may include music on radios and TVs in the background, or music that is performed by other characters during the game. Diegetic music is becoming more common in games as environments become more immersive, either as a means to enhance the environment, or to provide an interactive element. Radios are often used to add gravity to game sound environments, such as in *Portal* and in *Bioshock.* As the player approaches a lift in *Bioshock,* for example, a melody plays inside the lift. Because of the setting and the way the sound is used within the game to enhance the environment, these radios add a dimension to the realness. *Portal* contains no background music, only sound effects, and occasional dication from GLaDOS. However, there are radios throughout the game that do contain music. The presence or absence of these radios, as well as the lack of music elsewhere, gives their appearance more gravity and impact. Diegetic sounds can also be used for interactive elements, such as in *Minecraft*, where a player encounters radios and can select the sound. This sound selection also gives the player a feel of control over the environment.

6.11 Conclusion

The interactive nature of gameplay results in the need for music that has special qualities. Most of these qualities are derived from the unique requirement of game music to be unending, and for the lack of sound-picture lock that is present in film. Video games are just not capable of producing picture lock, except in FMV sequences, and even in those situations, it is not always precise. Terminology surrounding video game music is emergent, and varies depending on whether the source is academic, or industry-based. Unlike electroacoustic concert music, video game music lacks a unified body of scholarship surrounding it, and this

---

[78] See definition at Film Sound online, http://filmsound.org/terminology/diegetic.htm, accessed May 6, 2017.

text serves to provide a terminology that is accessible, and describes the music as it behaves functionally in game. Game interactivity does not mean automatically that the music is interactive, nor does infinite music mean that it is simply looping. As interactive media persists and continues to comprise a large portion of media consumption, this terminology may evolve and change. Many years ago most music was reactive, and generative music was not prevalent. Each generation of music presents its own series of challenges and musical needs, and this is also something that is unique to interactive media. In film, even though musical styles have vastly changed, musical function and purpose has not. It is also important to remember that not all of these terms are designed to describe video game music immutably, as there are continuums between them, and new games are being released that continuously challenge standards, especially in sound. However, knowing these terms allows you to apply them to music you are hearing in the games you play, and to further understand why there even may be a question of whether a piece of music is, for example, adaptive or interactive. These terms can also assist in the beginning of a conversation surrounding the unification between video game music scholarship and industry-focused publications.

Chapter 7: Form and Function of Game Music

Many of the characteristics of game music that we can hear today developed due to consistent and established paradigms in both game play and game sound. Early gameplay often followed a specific formula: the player finds/selects a level, then enters a level, player makes their way through obstacles in the level, and then returns to the selection area to progress to another level. This type of gameplay did not arise overnight, but rather evolved over time, and continues to evolve, as even the current games that are fully 3D involve different levels or stages throughout. This chapter examines some of the most common types of music for games and how the musical function relates to the area iwithin the game that the music is setting. Similarities in musical form, sound, mood, and instrumentation will be analyzed for areas such as overworld, underworld, battle, and theme. Also discussed in this chapter is genre-specific music. Just as different styles of music are required for different gameplay areas, different music is required for different genres of games, since the music needs to serve a different function to match the gameplay style. Therefore, the function of specific music in games is the primary focus of this chapter, and this is informed both by the musical style (i.e., rock-driven, ballad, orchestral) as well as the style of game play.

7.1 Basic Types of Game Music and Characteristics

Games began to develop structural similarities as they grew in popularity, and this continued as more advanced systems that could support longer and more complicated games hit the market. Early games had very distinct types of areas that continued to remain characteristic of games for many generations. These areas include levels or dungeons, battle areas, and zones outside of levels, commonly called overworlds. Artefacts of this early gameplay can be seen in modern games, although such distinct boundaries between areas became blurred with the advent of fully 3D environments. Some of the most particularly stylistic elements of game music emerged as a result of these areas within gameplay. The reason behind this is likely multifaceted, being perhaps informed by the desire to emulate popular games, common feelings regarding what kind of musical style evokes certain moods, and even player expectation (such as the expectation that all battle music will sound a certain way). The intention to clearly delineate areas is another possible reason. A discussion of these areas follows, including the type of gameplay that generally occurs and the style and character of the music alongside it. Music can contribute extensively to the overall tone and environment within the game, and can serve to engage the player or keep them entertained if they are in an area for a long time. The music therefore helps to inform or serve the gameplay in these situations, and there are many musical tools composers use to convey the nature of the area. The advancement of technological capabilities for gaming would see the development of more diverse collections of areas within games, and the music followed (this can also be seen in soundtrack length - compare the number of tracks in *Mario* to *Final Fantasy VI*!). For the purposes of this chapter, we will focus on the following key musical types to begin with: overworld, underworld, battle, safe zone, and theme. Each area discussion contains some examples from earlier game music (beginning from when the areas were clearly distinct from one another in gameplay) as well as examples from new video games that involve fully 3D environments and more gradual changes, so that we can trace the development and how it has changed over time. For the purposes of this section, platformer games, action-adventure games, and RPGs will be the primary focus, as they are most likely to contain these characteristic levels; the latter half of the chapter explores genre-specific music at length.

7.2 Overworld/Field

The term *overworld* is used in two respects in this text. First, as an area within a platformer outside of dungeons, caves, or other dark and low areas (i.e., not the underworld), and also as the main area that connects all the areas of gameplay (levels) within a game. The latter type of overworld is often seen in game genres such as adventure or RPGs, in which there is a large area, often referred to as a world map, that connects several other areas that players can enter. I also group **overworld** and **field** in the same category in this text because the two contain many similarities, both aesthetically and musically. Overworlds are intended to be expansive and vast, and are generally less ominous and dark in character than **underworlds** or **dungeons**, although they are not necessarily devoid of enemies. Often the scenery in an overworld includes nature: grass, trees, large landscape structures, and brightly coloured visuals. The music generally contains a similar aesthetic: the melodies tend to be positive and in a major key, the instrumentation tends to be light, with many strings (plucked and bowed) and occasionally wind instruments. Percussive instruments, if they are used, are generally higher pitched and most often hand percussion (or snare drums). The rhythms are steady and sometimes fast, but usually at a walking tempo, and jarring irregularities and syncopations in rhythm are not generally common. Finally, the form tends to be very open, with larger loops than in other areas and structural variance that gives the illusion of dynamic looping. Below we will examine three different overworld themes: "Overwold" from *Super Mario Bros.*, "Time's Grassland" from *Chrono Cross*, and the "Hyrule Field" theme from *The Legend of Zelda: Ocarina of Time*. These examples are discussed to demonstrate the qualities consistent to overworld music. Listen to these themes before and after reading the text to gain a greater understanding of how they serve to enhance and inform gameplay.

7.2.1 Overworld: Super Mario Bros. (1985), Koji Kondo

The overworld theme for the original Super Mario Bros. remains one of the most recognizable video game tunes to date.[79] This is the music that serves as soundtrack during the first level of the original *Super Mario Bros*. The level itself takes place in an outdoor side-scrolling environment, and involves Mario proceeding through the level, jumping on enemies, avoiding falls, and gathering items. The music replicates the expansiveness of the environment, even with the limited means allowed the composer because of the Nintendo's sound restrictions. Therefore, this track does not contain the typical orchestration described above, because Kondo was limited to the few additive synth channels available on the NES. However, Kondo manages to evoke the characteristics of overworld music through other means, including melodic structure, large-scale form, rhythmic content, and overall affect. The melody is catchy and light-hearted, with activated rhythms, short note durations, and a lot of counterpoint. The length of the theme itself is substantial, with a full loop lasting 1 minute and 30 seconds. While this is not by any means lengthy in comparison to streaming audio loops, this represents a substantial loop length for the 8-bit generation. Koji Kondo used a unique ordering of sections to perceptibly lengthen the loop, once again using limited musical material, but still managing to musically depict vast and open gameplay. The theme itself is broken down into smaller components, of which there are 4; I will give these components section letters from A-D, the letter name representing the first appearance of the section.

Therefore, if we assign these letters to the overall form of the piece, the resulting structure is:

A (4 bars) A (4 bars)
B (8 bars) B (8 bars)
C (8 bars)

---

[79] David, BJ. "Top 10 Most Recognizable Video Game Music Themes," GMA News Online, April 27, 2012, http://www.gmanetwork.com/news/story/256153/scitech/technology/top-10-most-recognizable-video-game-music-themes, accessed May 6, 2017.

A (4 bars) A (4 bars)
D (8 bars) D (8 bars)
C (8 bars)
D (8 bars)

As this formal examination demonstrates, not only does Kondo use a large amount of different melodic and rhythmic structures, but also they are ordered in such a way that a repetitive pattern cannot be determined within the loop. This evokes the concept of dynamic looping (although this is not a dynamic loop), a technique that would be explored later as a means to make loops less mundane and enhance gameplay.[80]

7.2.2 Overworld: "Time's Grasslands", Chrono Cross (1999), Yasunori Mitsuda

Chrono Cross was released on the PlayStation, and therefore the instrumental palette was more diverse and we do get a sense of the orchestrational techniques that are used to convey a sense of overworld. The instrumentation of "Time's Grassland" consists of light drums, some plucked strings, and a sitar that plays the melody. The concept of expansiveness is present within this as well, as the melody is quite long, and is actually a slightly slowed down version of the melody from the original *Chrono Trigger* theme. The overall rhythm of the piece remains consistently at a moderate walking tempo, with no syncopations or unexpected rhythmic changes. An acoustic plucked string instrument in the medium pitch register (likely a Mediterranean guitar) performs an arpeggiated figure at the same rhythmic structure consistently throughout, and the sitar melody remains at the foreground. The melody does not have a sense of urgency, and gives the track a sense of meandering or wandering, which is also appropriate for an overworld or field soundtrack. The simplicity of the selection is also important - the instrumentation is very light, and the *Chrono Trigger* theme is the only present melodic element. There is no counterpoint, secondary section, or intense orchestrational layering. Unlike the *Super Mario* overworld theme, Time's Grasslands has a very simple form, and doesn't transition to a B section; rather, the melody just repeats over and over on top of the walking tempo backdrop, to create a sense of endless exploration.

---

[80] Sweet, Michael. *Writing Interactive Music for Video Games: A Composer's Guide.* Pearson Education, 2014.

7.2.3 Overworld: "Hyrule Field", Legend of Zelda: Ocarina of Time, Koji Kondo

Hyrule field, like many overworld/field areas, consists visually of trees, grassy hills, dirt pathways, and expansive scenery and skies. Much like "Time's Grasslands", the music involves some elements and references to the original (in this case) Zelda theme through the use fragmented melodic excerpts. The music remains consistently at a moderate to fast tempo, and contains a steady rhythm without irregularities or syncopations. Link encounters enemies on this field, but unlike in RPG games of the same generation, there is no transition to battle screen and Link battles enemies on the field freely. This may also contribute to the more heroic, fast rhythms in this particular field theme, as well as some of the intense and dissonant sections of the music. It is generally engaging and lengthy, and this long loop length (almost 5 minutes) also illustrates the expansiveness of the area. The orchestration consists primarily of held string instruments, with snare drums, wind instruments, and higher brass instruments. This is a common orchestration set for field music, and the addition of horns and snare drums give a militaristic sense to the music, which is also another product of the musical function: this occurs during an area where Link battles enemies with no musical or visual transition. Therefore, the music must serve to illustrate expansiveness, engage the player, and be appropriate for battle situations.

7.3 Underworld/Dungeon

The term **underworld** will be used in this text to describe those areas or levels in which the player is underground, in a cave or dungeon, or any other enclosure that contains frequent encounters with enemies. **Underworld** and **dungeon** are both acceptable terms that can be used to describe these areas. Often, and especially in RPGs, characters cannot save at any point while in an underworld (this is possible on world map overworlds). Dungeons and underworlds represent one of the earliest paradigms of game levels, emerging out of the tradition of a player selecting and entering a dungeon from a larger world to "crawl." Today such levels are incredibly diverse, spanning many different types of areas conceptually and visually. Additionally, as games become more and more open world, such level music becomes more ambiguous and varied. Therefore, we will also examine the evolution of underworld music by evaluating extremely early (8-bit) games, as well as very recent games. There were clear transitions between the overworld area and the underworld in the earlier games. However, more recent games will often have a musical change in a more seamless manner when, for example, the character enters a room where there are enemies, or when the enemies approach the character. There are many musical characteristics that are common of underworld music: it tends to be less colourfully orchestrated than overworld music, generally lower in pitch, contains sparser orchestration, less fluid melodies, and shorter loops (or perceptibly shorter loops). All of these elements help to portray the sense of restriction within dungeons. Often jarring rhythmic devices and irregular melodies are used to give the player a sense of danger, or imminent threat.

7.3.1 Dungeon: Super Mario Bros., Koji Kondo

Mario and Luigi, the characters from the original *Super Mario Bros.*, are plumbers by profession, and the game creators therefore decided to use pipes as a transportation device within the game. The underworld is reached through the transportation through one of these pipes, and this underworld is no exception to the characteristics of such levels. The underworld in *Super Mario* is dark and sparsely coloured, and the scenery consists of dark blue bricks against a black backdrop. The music is also a very representative example of some of the stylistic components frequently used in dungeon music: the melody is memorable but not singable, relying on a rhythmic motive rather than a lengthy melodic theme. The sound is low in pitch, and less contrapuntally dense than the overworld theme. There are no white-noise drums in the background, and a singular square wave line is the sole instrument in the mix. The theme consists of a short monophonic (solo) line: a rhythmic motive repeated twice, then transposed down in pitch and repeated twice, then finally followed by a short spinning out of this motive. A short silence exists between the end of the loop and the beginning of the next, adding to the sensation of darkness, sparseness, and anticipation. The length of the loop is about 12 seconds, a considerable difference from the 1 minute and 30 seconds allocated to the overworld theme. The shortness of the loop, the restriction of the melody and instrumentation, and the lack of singable melody are all elements that give the piece a sense of enclosed space, drab colouring, and limitation.

7.3.2 Underworld: "Dungeon", Diablo (1996), Matt Uelmen

Diablo has been described as a hack and slash/RPG combination, but another term commonly used to describe such games is "dungeon crawl". A dungeon crawl is a gametype in which players proceed through a maze-like underworld (dungeon), and fight off enemies, usually stealing their treasure as well. *Diablo* involves the player navigating sixteen randomly generated dungeons and eventually entering Hell to defeat Diablo. Like many other RPGs, there are opportunities for the player to customize their character. The gameplay in *Diablo* is considerably different from *Mario Bros,* therefore, both in player mechanics and background story. The dungeon music for Diablo (titled appropriately, "Dungeon"), however, contains a lot of similar elements to the *Mario Bros.* underworld theme, with the primary exception being the loop length (*Diablo* was also released for PC, which had a substantially more advanced sound card). The track begins with a low, drone-like choir sound, and continues to remain in the lower pitch range throughout. Sounds fade in and fade out, and include bass drums, low brass, low strings, and some sound effects. The one exception to the very low-pitched material is the extremely high and dissonant strings that occur, which are present in the track. This device, however, has become idiomatic in the horror genre, and therefore its use also contributes to the sense of impending doom and constriction. Like the Mario theme, the *Diablo* underworld music is very sparsely orchestrated, usually with only 2-3 combinations of instruments at a time. Additionally, while there are some very low motivic elements that recur, there isn't really an expansive melody in this piece, and while the loop is long (over 4 minutes), the sounds are fragmented and short, much like the Mario theme.

7.3.3 Underworld: "Fish in a Barrel", Gears of War (2006), Kevin Riepl

Gears of War is a third-person shooter, and therefore has different gameplay mechanics than the games previously discussed in this chapter. However, the music functions similar to the dungeon music described in the previous two examples. "Fish in a Barrel" is slightly different from the other two examples because it does not score an underworld or enclosed dungeon, but rather occurs in an area where there is present danger. This represents one of the ways in which levels in games have evolved as more realistic worlds become possible to play in digitally. Rather than the player entering a new "scene", enemies approach the character within the 3D world that they are already present in. However, just like when entering a dungeon from an overworld, the track represents a transition from an area without danger to an area with present danger. The colouring of the game and the post-apocalyptic landscape makes the game visuals grey and neutral in colour, without any of the bright colours and cartoony realism present in earlier overworld areas. Examining this type of track is important because there are no transition screens or partitioned areas. In *Gears of War*, for example, enemies appear on a more continuous basis, as the player navigates through a fully immersive 3D environment. Therefore, unlike the Mario underworld music, which transitioned abruptly and accompanied a complete screen change, "Fish in a Barrel" begins playing as soon as the player is in a region where enemies are present and able to attack you, and remains until the player leaves this region, even though there may be no visual difference between regions. The musical transition is seamless. Despite all the differences in gameplay, however, this track contains many similarities to other underworld music: heavy low-pitched strings and brass, bass drums, short, rhythmic motives, and an absence of bright and expansive melodies. Therefore, even though many gameplay and design elements are different from the two examples from earlier generations, the artefacts from early video games remain present. They will likely continue to persist in the future, although in an evolved state.

7.5 Battle

While there are many different types of battle in games, for the purposes of this text, we will consider **battle** areas to be those areas in which the player is actively involved in battle. For a piece of music to be classified as battle music, the music must change to reflect these conditions. This is in contrast to the overworld music we studied from *Ocarina of Time*, in which Link freely engaged in battle with enemies on the field, without any changes in the music. Battle music is also different from underworld music because it occurs following a change from advancing through the level to engaging in battle. In an underworld, conversely, there can be enemies around you, but you may not be engaged with them. Occasionally there will be no battle music, and the level music will simply continue as the player fends off enemies, as we discussed above regarding *Ocarina of Time*. Early battle music often shared many characteristics of rock music and/or symphonic metal. A typical battle theme included either rock band instruments, such as guitars, keyboards, and drums, or symphonic instruments playing rock-inspired music. However, more recent battle music also contains cinematic influences, with the low brass, dissonant sonorities, and heavy drums that accompany more tense situations in recent film scores. Both styles are present, and tend to be linked to the genre of gameplay, as well as the overall sound palette of the soundtrack and visuals of the game.

7.5.1 Battle: Final Fantasy (1987), Nobuo Uematsu

The RPG battle theme is one of the most distinguishable types of video game music, having very particular characteristics that persist across (especially the earlier) titles, consoles, and developers. *Final Fantasy* was one of the earliest RPGs to feature a battle theme, and many of the qualities of this theme have influenced battle themes in RPGs through the current era. The original *Final Fantasy* was released for the NES, and therefore was limited to additive synthesis. The trademark of this track is the rock-inspired opening, with a strong, rhythmic motive that progresses into quick melodic elements. This battle theme contains two main sections: the first containing the fast rhythmic elements, and the second consisting of a slower melodic line, but also with a progressive rock-inspired rhythm. All of these features remained in later battle themes, and once the move was made away from the limitations of additive synthesis, many of these themes contained similar rhythmic motives in string sections, with other orchestral instruments accompanying. Others also use electric guitar, keyboard, and other rock instruments. Drums and rhythmic percussion remain prevalent regardless, as do many of the rock-inspired rhythms.

7.4.2 Battle: "Roar Of the Departed Souls", Lost Odyssey (2008), Nobuo Uematsu

Boss battle themes generally are similar in style to battle music, but larger in scope and length, and are usually associated with the character (or their incarnation) that you are fighting. Many boss fight themes have a fuller orchestration, although there is still a heavy rock influence, and quick repeating rhythmic gestures. Sometimes boss battle themes will incorporate an instrument (or instrument group) or musical theme that has been associated with the antagonist that is being fought, and "Roar of the Departed Souls" does contain excerpts from the antagonist's theme. The track occurs in *Lost Odyssey* when the characters are fighting the final boss, Gongora. Like many of Nobuo Uematsu's other major boss themes (such as "One-Winged Angel"), there are also choir sounds. This particular boss battle includes heavy electric guitar, spoken voice, choir, and full orchestral sounds, including the rhythmic strings and drums that are often present in regular battle music. Loop length for boss battles is commonly longer than normal battle music, with a larger number of differing sections. "Battle Theme", for example, contained a loop length of about 45 sections and two distinct sections, whereas "Roar of the Departed Souls" contains a lengthy intro, four sections, and a loop length of almost three minutes. This form difference is likely due to the expected length of battle, which is much longer for boss battles, and even more so for major boss battles such as Gongora.

7.4.3 Battle: "Battle Music I", Elder Scrolls: Skyrim (2013), Jeremy Soule

Skyrim, the fifth instalment in the Elder Scrolls series, is also an RPG, but with different battle mechanics, setting, and stylistic characteristics than previously-discussed RPGs such as *Final Fantasy* and *Lost Odyssey*. The musical response in *Skyrim* is very similar of that in *Gears of War*, as it behaves in an adaptive rather than reactive way. In this game, once you engage with enemies, the music changes seamlessly into a battle theme, with no visual screen change to battle scene. It does share many characteristics of other battle themes, however, including heavy use of drums and rhythmic string motives. There is also an addition of low brass tones, an orchestrational technique that has become idiomatic in film music. The melody is slightly different from, for example, Uematsu's battle themes, in that it is less overt and functions more as a background element. This may be a result of the immersive gameplay style, however, which often requires music to be more environmental and ambient, and less imposing on the already very cluttered visual and aural environment. While it might seem as if there is no difference between this music and the *Gears of War* track discussed above, the behaviour and musical function of both is actually quite different. "Fish in a Barrel", for example, activates and remains activated in an area even after the enemies are gone; the track will not change until the player enters another area. The *Elder Scrolls* music, in contrast, is tied to the battles themselves, and once the enemies are eliminated, the music seamlessly transitions away from the battle music.

7.5 Safe Zones

In many games there exist locations where a character cannot get into battle. Sometimes these areas are towns or villages, often where the characters get rest and gather information and items, but they may also be areas within a game in which the character has to complete some kind of puzzle-oriented task. Because of the less imminent threat of battle, music for safe zones tends to be calmer, with folk-like melodic themes, a slower rhythmic pace, and a lighter mood.

7.5.1 Safe Zones: "Return to Town", Final Fantasy VI, Nobuo Uematsu

Safe zones are prevalent in RPGs such as Final Fantasy, where a weary party will often need to get rest. In *Final Fantasy VI*, all towns had the same theme. This is not the case in later games, in which individual cities often have their own individual themes. Generally, these safe zones are locations that allow the players to get rest (restore health and magic points), stock up on items, gather information, and advance the story. The "Town Theme" in *Final Fantasy VI* is very characteristic of safe zones, with very light orchestration and a folk-like, singable melody. A plucked string instrument performs an arpeggiated gesture throughout, at a very steady and slow walking tempo. There is also a bowed string pad in the background, with melody played on a woodwind instrument. Notable is the lack of drums and the steadiness of the string arpeggiation, which gives the music a calm and serene affect. All of these elements are a result of the lack of immediate hostility that the character will encounter in the area. Safe zones in later games retain a lot of the same qualities as "Town Theme", although they become more individualized. Rather than a singular castle and town theme that plays anytime a party is in a location of either category, for example, each castle and town is given its own theme, that highlights unique qualities about the area. Safe zone themes therefore also often serve as characterizing themes for their respective areas.

7.6 Theme Music

Of all the types of game music we have examined thus far, theme music by far is the most diverse. This is because theme music is intentionally individual and must be distinct and identifiable. While the other musical types are intended to reflect areas within the game, and although they often contain themes that are modified versions of character or story themes (something that will be discussed later), theme music is intended to create a musical "brand" or identity for the game. The goal of theme music is to be as distinct as possible, so that players will easily recognize and identify the game just by hearing the music. Three themes are examined below, each of which is quite different from each other. There is no characteristic orchestration, style, or mood present in theme music as in the other types of music that we discussed. However, recently theme music for many video games is beginning to follow certain established idioms and paradigms from cinematic title music, especially in form and orchestration.

7.6.1 Theme Music: Metroid (1986), Hip Tanaka

The theme music for *Metroid* (1986) is one of the most influential title tracks, not only because Hip Tanaka took a novel approach, but because many contemporary games sought to emulate the music for *Metroid*. The game takes place on a different planet and follows the protagonist, Samus, as she attempts to prevent Space Pirates from eventually taking over and destroying any opposing forces, including herself. The theme music sought to combine non-musical as well as musical elements, blurring the distinction between the two and allowing sound effects to function as musical elements.[81] This was difficult on the NES due to the

---

[81] Brandon, Alexander. "Shooting from the Hip: An Interview with Hip Tanaka."

limited amount of channels, but Tanaka managed to use the synthesized sounds to emulate sound effects, with careful consideration given to pitch trajectory and space between notes. A singular repeated low pitch is all that is heard in the beginning for example, followed by some higher sounds. The lack of melodic or rhythmic trajectory aids in allowing the sounds to emulate sound effects (or non-musical soundtrack elements). Tanaka's choice to use this technique as a means to add game atmosphere to the soundtrack was incredibly important to theme music, because it encouraged others to later create very individual themes that evoked the mood or storyline of the game. His use of sound effect-inspired sounds and sparse musical composition easily illustrated the game's relation to outer space and character isolation. It also represents a composition for NES that doesn't involve some of the common characteristics of Nintendo sound, including very short notes and dense counterpoint. Tanaka used counterpoint, but crafted the theme carefully so that it had a distinct sound.

7.6.2 Theme Music: "To Zanarkand", Final Fantasy X, Nobuo Uematsu

While there are several Final Fantasy games with excellent theme songs, I am choosing to discuss "To Zanarkand" because it represents a stylistic departure from other Final Fantasy themes, and demonstrates how diverse title and theme music can be. The music consists of a piano solo, with a slow melody backed by legato arpeggiated chords. The title music illustrates the opening sequence effectively: the characters begin the game sitting around a fire, surrounded by ruins. The main character, Tidus, states "Listen to my story. This… may be our last chance."[82] Like many RPGs, the characters are on a quest to save the world from a destructive force. The piano music, being limited in instrumentation with a melancholy, somber affect, evokes the nostalgic and somewhat sad elements of the game. *Final Fantasy X* does have a successful ending in that (so long as the player succeeds) the characters to manage to avert impending world destruction, but discoveries about the main character prevent the ending from being happy. This theme is also a good example of a successful title theme that does not follow the cinematic convention of sustained strings, brass, and repetitive thematic melody. Uematsu uses a nothing but singular instrument to set the opening of the game, and manages with this limited means to effectively evoke the overall affect of the game.

---

http://www.gamasutra.com/view/feature/2947/shooting_from_the_hip_an_.php, accessed May 6, 2017.

[82] *Final Fanasy X*, Square-Enix, 2001.

7.6.3 Theme Music: Halo: Combat Evolved (2001), Martin O'Donnell/Michael Salvatori

Halo was revolutionary in its FPS gameplay, and would have an effect on subsequent FPS releases. The music and sound of *Halo* was equally revolutionary, and Martin O' Donnell and Michael Salvatori contributed immensely through their work on the *Halo* soundtrack to interactive sound in games, use of theme in games, and sound design in general. The *Halo: Combat Evolved* theme becomes an integral part of entire soundtrack, with elements of this theme fragmented and distributed into almost every track on the soundtrack (this will be discussed at length in the next chapter). Once again demonstrating the diversity of title music, the theme for *Halo* includes Gregorian-like chant melody, which is followed by a rock-inspired, rhythmic drum and string line. This theme then functions in two ways: 1) to set up the "characterization" of the enemy, as the covenant are highly religious, hence the inclusion of chant, and 2) to provide a musical backdrop that engages and activates the player, and the drums and strings serve this function well.

7.7 Conclusion and More Types of Game Music

The sections above only discuss certain types of music that tend to persist over several genres, and are very common in many games. However, this is not an exhaustive examination, and there are several other area types in games, especially as games become more expansive and include more diverse level types, and smoother transitions between areas or situations in the game. Genre also has a significant effect on musical style, and there are many specific genres of games that do not contain music that falls into the categories discussed above (such as racing or fighting games). The diversity of gaming in every aspect is only increasing, and this includes level types and game genres (and sub-genres). This chapter will therefore continue with a discussion of some of the genre-specific music that we haven't discussed yet, and how it functions to serve its genre.

7.8 Genre-specific Music Characteristics

Much of the music discussed above does fall into the category of some of the genres discussed below, so the discussion will focus primarily on the types of music we did not cover, as well as more extensive focus on the genres that the music discussed above is not applicable to. Genres are continuously being developed, and new genres and subgenres do emerge, therefore it is beyond the score of this text to discuss music for all game genres in depth. This section is intended to provide you with a brief introduction to the purpose of music in games, and how music functions in a broad variety of game genres.

However, before we proceed we must answer the question: what exactly is a genre? This is a term often applied to music (i.e., pop, rock, classical) as well as video games (First-person shooter, adventure, RPG, etc.). William Hughes defines literary genre as the following:

> The division and grouping of texts on the basis of formal, thematic, or stylistic criteria. Texts may be produced, it can be argued, in compliance with or against the strictures of an established and identifiable genre, though it is equally feasible to impose a genre identity upon a work in retrospect, thus attributing to it further possibilities of meaning or, conversely, limiting its potential signification. In literature, genre lacks universal boundaries. The same might be said for other cultural practices in which genre is the primary mode of division—art, music, and cinema providing obvious parallels.[83]

In his thesis "The Fundamentals of Video Game Music Genre," David Lawrence Newcomb asserted regarding this definition that "the imposition of a genre is theoretical because its definition relies on wide acceptance among listeners, critics, artists, and scholars."[84] This is also applicable to video game genres themselves, as there are no academically established definitions, and games are released within generally accepted genres. Game genre is primarily a response to the gameplay mechanics, rather than the aesthetics of the game, although aesthetics tend to persist across genres. It is also important to note that genres are continuously evolving. Steve Horowitz states in *The Essential Guide to Game Audio* that "game mechanics and genres are constantly in flux and many designers will often combine elements of several of these types of gameplay. If the game sells well, it can sometimes become a genre or style by itself that can then be copied or adapted further by others. It's all part of the evolution of games."[85] For the purposes of this text, we will consider the definition of game genre that relates to the mechanics of gameplay. The genres described below represent a only a selection of

---

[83] William Hughes, Maryanne Cline Horowitz, ed. "Genre," *New Dictionary of the History of Ideas 3* (2005): 912-918.

[84] Newcomb, David Lawrence. *The Fundamentals of the Video Game Music Genre.* James Madison University, 2012.

[85] Horowitz, Steve, and Scott R. Looney. *The Essential Guide to Game Audio: The Theory and Practice of Sound for Games.* CRC Press, 2014.

current game genres, as well as a description of how the music functions within them.

7.8.1 Action, Adventure, and Action-adventure

Several types of action and adventure games contain the music described above, especially platformer games, adventure games, 3D adventure games. Therefore, this section will focus on shooting games and action games. Shooting games tend to have music that is fast-paced, and often inspired by rock or techno music. Winifred Phillips proposed that musical genres and game genres were often paired because of common preferences: "we look at the specific game genres that these player types enjoy most, and we'll begin to see connections forming between preferred music styles and preferred game genres."[86] Phillips concludes that this is partially due to a personality alignment with the people that enjoy genres such as rock, and genres such as shooters. However, it could also be attributed to gameplay: FPS games require quick thinking and fast action on part of the player, and rock music provides an engaging backdrop that keeps the players alert. FPS games also contain a large quantity of sound effects as well as visual displays that the player has to pay attention to and respond to. Therefore, thematic content may not be discernible in the same way as in games with a lower continuous aural sound effect load. However, the music does need to keep the player engaged and activated for fighting. This applies also to beat 'em ups, such as *God of War* or *Dante's Inferno* (2010), both action-adventure games in which the player often fights large quantities of enemies at a single time, and there is much information that the player has to keep track of on screen. The music in these games tends to be more environmentally reflective than in shooters, often evoking time periods or cultures, but this is also likely due to the fact that shooters are often set in contemporary and/or realistic environments.

7.8.2 Role-Playing Games

Since role-playing games were discussed extensively earlier in this chapter, this section will not go into too much detail. However, it is important to understand the structure of RPG soundtracks. RPG soundtracks are some of the most expansive game soundtracks in existence, with games often containing several character themes, as well as main game themes, battle music, boss music, and often a pop-ballad song that will become a hit (although this trend has primarily taken off in Japan). The music in RPGs is diverse, as the game generally encompasses an entire world, and thus, there are themes for island towns,

---

[86] Phillips, Winifred. *A Composer's Guide to Game Music*. MIT Press, 2014, p 83.

themes for forests, themes for underground caves, and many other areas. RPG soundtracks contain cultural influences, historical influences, and influences from film. However, the most important thing to understand regarding the function of RPG music is that it is used to create an environment or a world, and that includes atmospheric qualities of music, as well as character and location themes. The music in RPGs is often so present and expansive that it becomes an integral component of the gameplay, much like the storyline.

7.8.3 Strategy Games
The genre of **strategy games** includes all games that require considerable thinking ahead and strategic moves during gameplay. Like all of the other genres, there exists several types of strategy games, including tower defense games, turn-based strategy games, tactical games, and many others. Strategy games are very commonly played online, and can be real-time or than turn-based. Two such strategy games are the Civilization series, which is turn-based, and the Age of Empires series, which is a real-time strategy game. Both games are set against a historical background, and involve the player building and defending a civilization. The primary difference between the two, however, is the gameplay mechanics, specifically regarding whether the players take turns selecting actions or continuously select actions. The result is a change in pace of gameplay. The perspective in both remains similar to that in a lot of "God games," as the player has a bird's eye view of the field. The music for both games contains references to ethnic and historical instruments, likely due to the historical setting of these games. These include instrumental references, choral references, melodic references, and many other stylistic traits of the historical period or civilisation that the player is in at a given moment. Earlier versions of Civilization and Age of Empires had very similar soundtrack designs, with primarily looping non-diegetic music. The more recent iterations in both series tend to contain more sound effects, with the musical soundtrack having less of a presence. However, the point of view remains the same, and these games do not function the same way that AAA third-person action adventure titles do. The player is more removed from the playing field, rather than being immersed in it. Like many other genres of games, this is changing, but strategy games generally involve a lot of time away from the active engagement in battle, with building, constructing, and gathering materials being a key component to the gameplay. Strategy games are considered to have emerged out of the concept of board gaming; if you imagine a game of Chess, there is a considerable amount of thinking and planning that goes on before a

player makes an actual move. As such, the music reflects this concept, and unlike in shooter games or fighter games where the music provides an environmental component against a heavy sound effect backdrop, music in strategy games tends to be more present and thematic, especially when the player is involved in the planning stage. This changes when the player enters a fighting situation, as now the player has to manage many different sources of feedback on screen to respond to.

7.8.4 Sports Games

Sports games haven't been discussed extensively in this text because the music functions so differently within them, including at some points not at all. Nevertheless, it is important to study the use of sound and music in sports games because they make up a large market share of the video game industry, and sound is actually a very important crucial component in these games. For the most part, there is no continuous background soundtrack in sports games. However, the intent of sports games is to be incredibly realistic, and playing a sports game almost entirely reflects an interactive experience of watching a sporting event on TV. For example, in FIFA games, there is some background music in certain areas away from gameplay, such as during some of the career mode menu screens. However, during the game, non-diegetic sound is removed, and the soundtrack (or more accurately, soundscape) includes the sounds of the crowd, sounds of the ball and players, and the commentators. Musical cues and alerts are heard, just as one would hear either on TV watching the event or if they were a spectator in the arena. Occasionally music is present, but this is diegetic music that is also heard by the crowd and the players. This style of sound environment is genre-specific; these realistic team sports games are targeting a very specific audience that is looking for a replication of a sporting event. Some sporting games, however, use music to evoke the culture or subculture that surrounds the event. An example of this would be *Tony Hawk's Pro Skater*, a skateboarding game that was endorsed by pro skater Tony Hawk. Skateboarding has often been considered to be a part of the punk subculture, and a large portion of this culture includes the listening to certain types of music, often referred to collectively as "punk music".[87] Therefore the choice to use licensed music, and more particularly, a specific genre of licensed music, was also intended as a way to brand the game with this particular subculture, targeting a specific audience. This music doesn't necessarily serve for a realistic or immersive purpose, but rather to engage the player

---

[87] Ensminger, David. *Visual Vitriol: The Street Art and Subcultures of the Punk and Hardcore Generation*, University Press of Mississippi, 2011, p. 107

(the music is upbeat), and to bring the player into the subculture of skateboarding, complete with the type of music skateboarding is often associated with.

7.8.5 Fighting Games

Fighting games were popularized in the arcade era, being a perfect gameplay type for two friends that wanted to play against each other, since they involve each player controlling a singular character onscreen that fights the other character on screen. The popularity of fighting games decreased somewhat in the 1990s as home consoles became more advanced, but adding special attacks and storylines to games somewhat helped to re-popularize the genre. This did not seem to revive the genre entirely, however, and many criticized the growing complexity of fighting games as being a reason for the decrease in popularity.[88] Music for fighting games varies, depending on the level of immersion, style of gameplay, and environment. Fighting games that emulate sports (such as wrestling) are often realistic, like other sports games, and consist primarily of diegetic sounds. *Virtua Fighter,* a Sega title, incorporates non-diegetic music, allotting every player character an individual theme. When fighting with that character, the theme music plays in the background. Each of the themes has a very fast-paced rock/pop sound, although some themes attempt to illustrate the overall affect the creators intended to apply to the character. Soundtracks in fighting games tend to either be made up of character themes, or location themes (i.e., each stage or location a fight takes place on has its own musical theme). *Dead Or Alive 3,* released on Xbox did incorporate some character narrative, and each character had their own individual storyline, which the player could progress through in a narrative mode. Narrative became more common in later iterations of fighting games as they sought to reclaim their popularity, and exist on a larger scale like other console titles.[89] Unlike *Virtua Fighter,* the music in *Dead or Alive 3* is more characteristic of the Xbox generation, containing many diegetic sounds, and a fairly equal balance in volume between sound effects and music. The music does retain the activated rhythmic qualities of *Virtua Fighter,* as well as the character theme organization of tracks. The function of music in fighting games therefore remains primarily to keep the player engaged in the onscreen fight, although character and location association through the use of themes is also important.

---

[88] McLaughlin, Rus. "IGN Presents the History of *Street Fighter*." Imagine Games Network online, Feb 16, 2009, http://www.ign.com/articles/2009/02/16/ign-presents-the-history-of-street-fighter, accessed May 6, 2017.

[89] *Dead or Alive* (series), Koei Tecmo, 1996-2016.

7.8.5 Casual and Other Games

The music for casual games is diverse in content, because there is such a wide body of casual games available. However, in general, casual games are intended for playing in short durations with little long-term time commitment or during parties. Therefore, the music tends to be light-hearted, with many loops, light orchestration, and catchy melodies. Especially since so many casual games are for iDevices with a finite amount of storage space, it is extremely common to see the technique of vertical re-orchestration in casual games. Many casual games contain no music, as in one of the original casual games, solitaire, as well as some other common early computer games, like Backgammon. Casual gaming has recently become a very large part of the market share, fuelled by the release of the Wii and iOS applications, and applications and downloadable games have essentially nearly taken over this market.[90] Mobile apps also present another limiting musical consideration, as iDevices are limited in volume and frequency reproduction due to their speaker size.

7.9 Dynamic Forms and Genres

There are several game types and types of music that do not fit into any of the categories discussed above, especially as new types of gameplay and new paradigms are continuously evolving. However, it is important to understand how the function of game music has evolved as it relates to the gameplay, and if we trace this historically, it is apparent that there are several consistencies. Such consistencies even persist into the current generation, although the examples are not as clear-cut once music becomes more adaptive (compare *Elder Scrolls* to *Gears of War,* for example). Visuals follow a similar paradigm; while players once waited for a new screen to load upon entering a new area, they are now free to roam fully 3D environments seamlessly. The music must functionally reflect that, and this is apparent in the *Gears of War* and *Elder Scrolls* examples. Music also is reflective of its genre and the type of gameplay that exists within it. This is driven both by marketing reasons as well as practical and aesthetic ones. Additionally, many of the stylistic characteristics that are genre-specific have come to be expected by the audience, and so some music for certain genres continues to retain stylistic qualities across console generations.

---

[90] Gaudiosi, John. "Mobile game revenues set to overtake console sales in 2015." Fortune online, Jan 15, 2015, http://fortune.com/2015/01/15/mobile-console-game-revenues-2015/, accessed May 6, 2017.

7.10 Conclusion

Music serves a function and purpose in video games, beyond the superficial intent of obtaining and retaining players. Music informs gameplay, and gameplay informs music. Certain musical characteristics are apparent in certain gameplay areas, as well as certain genres of game. These characteristics have grown out of gameplay traditions that used music to engage the player, and to express the environment and character of a particular point in the game. As games become more immersive, the boundaries between levels become blurred, as do the boundaries between sound and what the character can hear. Immersive and realistic games are more likely to contain diegetic sound and/or music components, and often these diegetic sounds are more present in volume than the non-diegetic music. Conversely, games that are less realistic and immersive, such as retro games, puzzle games, and turn-based games, have very present non-diegetic sound and music. Sound effects in these also games tend to be less realistic, and don't overpower the non-diegetic sounds in the game as they do in fully 3D and immersive games. There are therefore many demonstrable effects of musical function on musical sound in games.

Chapter 8: Characterization and Storytelling Using Themes

Advancements in technology have allowed games to possess increasingly extensive storylines and extremely developed characters. The design, characterization, and narratives in games has led many to argue that video games are one of the most important art forms of the digital age.[91] As a result of such detailed storylines and characters, game music has become more integral to the narrative process, just as it has in films. This chapter examines one such game, *Final Fantasy IX* (2000), and its use of character themes and thematic development as a means to aid characterization and narrative. Scored by Nobuo Uematsu, *Final Fantasy IX* contains an extensive soundtrack, including over 150 tracks. A background discussion regarding how themes are developed in movies and operas begins this chapter, followed by how these techniques inform the use of such themes in video games. Several key themes in *Final Fantasy IX* are analyzed, with emphasis placed on the location in which they appear in the game and how the adaptation of these themes serves the storyline. Following this, we examine the variation and re-use of a singular theme in several tracks of a video game. This technique is compared to art music's "cyclic form," a type of thematic treatment involving the use of a singular theme in many movements of a multi-movement work. We will see how cyclic form functions within the game *Halo: Combat Evolved* (2001) through an examination of how the main theme is integrated into nearly all of the tracks in the soundtrack.

8.1 Brief Background

The term leitmotif has been defined as a "short, constantly recurring musical phrase" associated with a particular person, place, or idea.[92] The German word translates to "leading motive." Generally, a leitmotif needs to be so distinct in rhythm, harmony, or melody that it can sustain transformation and remain distinguishable. The term is most often associated with Wagnerian opera, but Wagner was not the only composer to use it. "Leitmotif" is used almost interchangeably with "theme" presently, especially regarding film and video game music. However, it is essential to understand that what sets a leitmotif apart from the more general concept of theme is that a leitmotif retains its identifiability

---

[91] Tucker, Abigail. "The Art of Video Games," Smithsonian, March 2012, http://www.smithsonianmag.com/arts-culture/the-art-of-video-games-101131359/?no-ist, accessed May 6, 2017.

[92] Michael Kennedy, *The Concise Oxford Dictionary of Music*, Oxford, 1987, Leitmotif.

despite transformation. For the purposes of this text, we will define a **leitmotif** as a constantly recurring musical segment that is a associated with a particular person, place, or idea that retains its distinction through narrative transformations. However, when we refer to the more general thematic group of pieces that consist of music referring to a character or place, we will refer to that as a **theme.** The idea of **leitmotif** is almost taken for granted by our 21st century ears. During films, theatres, operas, musicals, and many other media, themes are present everywhere, and are an integral part of music's role in such media. This was not always so; for example, in an 18th century opera (such as Mozart) music would have been used to depict the emotion and drama within each scene, but themes were not necessarily associated with singular characters or ideas to the extent that can be seen in entertainment today. In contrast, a theme such as the "Imperial March" in *Star Wars* is associated with a character (in this case Darth Vader), and the appearance of a theme can foreshadow a character's appearance (the theme begins before we see the character, so we know he/she is coming), or even illustrate character growth (through minor changes in orchestration, mood, tempo, etc.). This concept is present in games as well, with both protagonists and antagonists having associated motives and themes that recur during moments in the game associated with these characters and their story arcs. Transforming such themes can be useful to create a sense of character progression, or to depict the emotional gravity of a situation a character is in. We will discuss this throughout the chapter, using the character and storyline development within the game *Final Fantasy IX*.

8.2 *Final Fantasy IX* (2000): Context

Final Fantasy IX was released for PlayStation in 2000 by Squaresoft, and represented the last instalment of the series for the original PlayStation. The game was released quietly, with substantially less hype than *Final Fantasy VII* and *VIII* (both were promoted for their then revolutionary graphics, length, and detailed story and gameplay). *Final Fantasy IX* represented a return to the medieval-style setting, including castles and dungeons, which a portion of the fan base had missed in the tech and futuristic-heavy *Final Fantasy VII* and *VIII*. The setting of the game is described on the Unofficial Final Fantasy Site:

> The epic tale of *Final Fantasy IX* takes place in the world of Gaia. Gaia is home to four great kingdoms: Lindblum, Alexandria, Burmecia and Cleyra. These kingdoms have, up until this point, always been at peace. Strange things are happening in Alexandria Castle however...there is talk of a strange man wandering the

corridors, and the Queen herself seems to be uneasy. War is brewing. The beautiful Princess of Alexandria, Princess Garnet Til Alexandros XVII, suspects evil intentions of this new person wandering the castle. With Royal Pendant in hand, she devises a plan to escape the castle by hitching a ride on the theater ship that will perform on her birthday.[93]

Unknown to Garnet, there were already plans in the works to kidnap the princess by the main character of the game, Zidane, Tribal, and members of his theatre group/band of thieves. Like many other main characters in RPGs, Zidane's origins are mysterious and end up becoming an integral plot point, which will be discussed below. The Princess, Zidane, and several other characters join forces in the game, each with his/her own motivation for saving the planet and fighting the "strange man" described above, who is the primary antagonist, named Kuja.

8.3 Terra's Theme

This section discusses a number of themes that come to be associated with Terra, a twin world that exists within Gaia, the world the characters live in. The characters are unaware of this world, although one of the main characters in *Final Fantasy IX*, Zidane, as well as the primary villain, Kuja, was actually created by the ruler of Terra as a crucial component to his plan to assimilate the two worlds.

8.3.1 "The Place I'll Return to Someday"

"The Place I'll Return to Someday" is heard during the title sequence, when the player first boots up the game. This interpretation of the theme is sparsely orchestrated, with two recorders performing the melody in counterpoint. It contains some characteristics of Renaissance or early Baroque music, written in a dance meter (although somewhat slow), and contains a simple formal structure, consisting of two contrasting sections (A and B). Normally, a dance would include the A section repeating at the end to form a ternary sectional form, but because this track is already looping, this type of repetition would be redundant. The contrapuntal writing of the recorders could also be interpreted as historically (Renaissance or Baroque) stylistic writing. The nature of this track, given its instrumentation, form, and genre, evokes a sense of nostalgia. This is further reinforced by the title, "The Place I'll Return to Someday", indicating that the place in question is possibly a memory or a place from the past. As we will see following our examination, Terra's theme has

---

[93] *"Final Fantasy IX*: Story," Unofficial Final Fantasy Site, http://www.uffsite.net/ff9/story.php, accessed May 6, 2017.

strong association to Zidane. Therefore, the nostalgic affect of the track also highlights Zidane's attitude that a "home is where the heart is" and a place where one can return to any time (referenced in the *Final Fantasy IX Ultimania*.)[94] Remembrance and belonging are recurring themes throughout the game, and this is especially explored through the use of musical themes. It is also notable that "The Place I'll Return to Someday" occurs at the title screen, which as we learned from a previous chapter, results in this melody functioning as the primary theme of the game, setting the overall tone of the game and cementing its importance.

8.3.2 "Oeilvert"

"Oeilvert" serves as location music for the Oeilvert area and contains Terra's theme. In this instance, the theme group is lacking the Renaissance dance reference that was present in the title theme, instead containing a plucked string accompaniment and some kind of drone instrument alongside a wind instrument that performs the melody. This track does not contain the contrapuntal elements as in the title track, and possesses heterophonic texture (a texture containing many textural variations of the same melodic line). As such, this track is much more evocative of ancient music, including instruments and playing styles associated with the Ancient Near East or Greece, such as heterophony and lyre (or other plucked string instrument) accompaniment. This historical style is representative of the location in which the theme occurs. Oeilvert is an ancient struction that contains Terran artifacts and history. Therefore, the historical references used in the music adequately depict the location. Additionally, this represents the use of foreshadowing, when the title of the main theme ("The Place I'll Return to Someday") is taken into consideration. "Oeilvert" contains Terra's Theme, and much of the information we discover at Oeilvert is related to Terra. For Zidane, Terra is the place he comes from, a place that according to his beliefs discussed above, he may return someday. This also establishes the theme as one that may be associated with Terra, and we later discover that the Terra's Theme melody is also within the Terra location music.

8.3.3 "Ipsen's Castle"

The party must locate mirrors at Ipsen's Castle in order to find passage to Terra. The castle, like Oeilvert, lies on the Forgotten Continent, and has architecture that is puzzling, including passageways that are sideways, upside down, and a maze-like interior. The Final Fantasy Ultimania describes Ipsen's Castle as "one of the locations from Terra that ended

---

[94] *Studio BentStuff,* Final Fantasy IX *Ultimania*. Square Enix, 2004, pp. 08-09.

up on Gaia 5000 years ago due to Garland's failed attempt to merge the two planets into one."[95] Ipsen's castle also has an effect on weapons in which the weaker weapons are actually more powerful, and the strongest weapons become the weakest. The music reflects all of these strange elements of the castle, and expectedly contains Terra's theme, which is performed on a recorder in the track. Once again, this location is related to Terra in some way, as it is a necessary step on the characters' journey to the planet, and is an important part of Terran (and Gaian) history. Terra's theme is transformed into a fragmented and compound melody that transitions later into a canon or round, which is a type of counterpoint that involves multiple instruments (or voices) performing the melody, each separated from the others by specific time intervals.[96] Choir sounds are present in the background as well, unlike in "The Place I'll Return to Someday." The fragmentation of the melody and more eclectic instrumentation reflect accurately the unusual setting of Ipsen's Castle.

8.3.4 "Terra"

When the characters finally arrive on Terra, they are greeted with a location music containing instruments such as harps, oboe, bells, and strings. Embedded within this location music is Terra's theme, performed on oboe and a type of synthesized bell, likely emulating a glockenspiel or other pitched percussion instrument. There is no reference to dance metre or historical music of any kind. The nostalgia and distance created by the historical references is removed, and instead the music evokes the present with a modern orchestral instrumental subset. Instruments such as strings, harps, and bells are often used in other media to represent celestial, or heavenly, elements; this also helps to give the track an otherworldly mood. We also discover during our visit in Terra that Zidane was created on Terra, which is perhaps why Terra's theme is "The Place I'll Return to Someday."

8.3.5 "Bran Bal"

The track "Bran Bal" is also a location theme for a place on the planet Terra. This track does not contain Terra's theme, but I am discussing it because the instrumental group used is the same as the one in "Terra", which establishes this instrumental group as being related to the planet. The harp strums used in the Bran Bal theme are taken directly from the

[95] Ibid.

[96] Johnson, David. 2001. "Round". *The New Grove Dictionary of Music and Musicians*, second edition, edited by Stanley Sadie and John Tyrell. London: Macmillan Publishers.

Terra location theme, but with a new melody in the background. This consistency of instrumentation and some of the musical qualities associates them with Terra. However, it also allows Terra's theme to be solely associated with Terra as an idea, a memory, or an origin unknown to a character, rather than a realized location – when the characters arrive at the main city/town in Terra, Bran Bal, Terra's theme is absent.

8.3.6 Summary
The melody that is discussed in this section, Terra's theme, occurs first during the main theme, titled "The Place I'll Return To Someday," and this title alludes to Zidane's unknown heritage. Terra may be a place of origin for Zidane, but he does not remember it, and the historical characteristics of the title theme evoke a sense of nostalgia. The theme itself is also present at the title screen, but serves very little function elsewhere in the game, until the characters are actively proceeding towards Terra. At this point Terra's theme is primarily used in location themes that contain information about Terra or are on the way to Terra. The melody undergoes several transformations, including orchestrational as well as structural, but it is clear upon listening that the melody is retained through these transformations, sustaining its status as leitmotif. In this way, the theme serves to foreshadow in its appearance at the title screen, and its re-appearance at Terra provides a musical analogue to Zidane's discovery - the "finding" of something he "remembered."

8.4 Melodies of Life Theme
"Melodies of Life" is a pop-ballad song that appears in *Final Fantasy IX* during the ending sequence of the game. This type of song is characteristic of JRPGs, appearing as early as the 16-bit area in *Tales of Phantasia* (Motoi Sakuraba), and being a feature of several other Final Fantasy games as well ("Eyes on Me" in *Final Fantasy VIII* was a major pop hit in Japan). Elements from "Eyes on Me" appeared throughout the game in modified forms to trace a couple of characters' development' as well as their love stories. Much like this use of the pop-ballad theme in *Final Fantasy VIII*, many components of "Melodies of Life" are used throughout *Final Fantasy IX* as character and location themes, all of which allude to Garnet's heritage and a past she also cannot fully remember. Throughout this section, I refer to Theme Group A and Theme Group B from "Melodies of Life", which correspond to the melodies of the verses and chorus respectively.

8.4.1 "Crossing These Hills"
"Crossing These Hills" plays whenever the characters are on the world map, which, using the terms of the previous chapter, would make the

track an "overworld" theme. Many of the characteristics of the track are associated with overworld themes; the tempo is moderate and walking-paced, and the instrumentation is light, including plucked strings, a soft synth instrument, a wind instrument, and bowed strings. Theme group A from "Melodies of Life" is the primary melodic element in this track. However, the melody's presence in this world map theme indicates to the player early on in the game that this melody is a key feature, especially regarding the quest of the game, since the melody plays during a period of adventure and of searching for the next place to go. This equally parallels Garnet's searching and finding herself and coming of age.

8.4.2 "Garnet's Theme"

Garnet's theme, which also contains theme group A from the "Melodies of Life" theme, subtextually illuminates Garnet's importance to the story, as well as the prominence of her physical and mental journey in the game. This theme starts with an activated woodwind backdrop and a string accompaniment, and a synthesized bell sound performs Theme group A. The melody is completely present in this theme, only changed from its presentation in "Crossing These Hills" in instrumentation and accompaniment. This creates a connection between the world map, and concept of "journey", and Garnet, even if the player isn't consciously aware of it.

8.4.3 "Eiko's Theme"

The player character Eiko joins the party late in the game, but does play a key role in the story. Like Garnet/Dagger, Eiko is a descendent of the Summoner tribe. However, unlike Garnet, she has spent her life living in the deserted summoner village, Maidan Sari. Garnet lived far away from the village and did not know of her heritage, while Eiko is fully aware of it. Eiko's theme is slow, lightly orchestrated, and mellow, including plucked string instruments, bowed string instruments, and woodwinds. Theme group A is apparent, but slightly modified and in the background, of "Eiko's Theme". Additionally, it is clear that the harmonies are derived from this melody. As this melody is also used as the primary melody in "Garnet's Theme", it indicates that the two are related somehow, and this eventually becomes known to the player. Eiko is also a descendent of the lost summoner tribe, and has skills similar to Garnet's. Both actually have the same heritage, Garnet just does not fully remember.

8.4.4 "Song From Her Memory"

"Song From Her Memory" is a track that frequently plays while Dagger is experiencing a memory, and she describes this song as being something she remembers but she cannot remember from where. It begins with a slow harp intro, performing Theme group B. Following the harp intro, a solo singer vocalises the syllable "la", also performing the melody from Theme group B. There is reverberation placed on the singer's voice, creating the illusion of distance and memory. Garnet claims this song is part of her memory, and it is revealed later in the game that Garnet's birth mother is the source of this musical memory. This memory also represents part of Garnet's journey: the discovery of who she really is and where she is from.

8.4.5 "Melodies of Life"
This song combines both theme groups into one larger song with added lyrics. In this way, it is combining the character of the summoner, (Garnet/Dagger) with her memory. This song marks the only time the two melodies come together, representing a wholeness that has been achieved, as Dagger has discovered her past, and mysteries that the entire party were searching for have been solved. This song also is played during the conclusion of the game, further establishing its position as creating closure and connection. It should be noted that there exists a strong thematic thread connecting the "Place I'll Return to Someday" and "Melodies of Life", since both themes are associated with elements that remain in character's memory and of the characters having a faint but incomplete recollection of someplace they have come from. It also highlights the ideas of origin and home, which are both important concepts throughout the game.

8.5 Kuja's Theme
The characters spend the majority of the game fighting a mysterious villain named Kuja. Kuja's theme group consists of a chromatic melody and continuously shifting harmonic background. The result is a haunting and delicate theme, which adequately portrays Kuja's character: Kuja was created by Garland to assist in the blending of Gaia and Terra first, but was deemed flawed because he did not experience childhood, which hindered his development of a special, and required skill, called trance. Therefore, he was well aware that Zidane was created because he was insufficient, and this fact tortured him.[97]

8.5.1 "Kuja's theme"
"Kuja's Theme" contains piano only, consisting of triplet arpeggiated figures accompanying the chromatic melody shown above. The chordal content of the theme is elusive, with progressions that are not logical

[97] Final Fantasy IX *Ultimania*.

from a functional harmony standpoint (while a study of the harmony is beyond the scope of this text, which is aimed at a more broad readership, suffice to say that the progressions are atypical). Both hands are in rhythmic unison as well, limiting the possibility of counterpoint and resulting in a singular, simple rhythmic design. The resulting sparse sound, coupled with the elusive harmonies, portrays the dark and delicate nature of Kuja, who is repeatedly referred to as "mystery man", and described as being "that mysterious figure around the castle".[98]

8.5.2 "Wicked Melody"

"Wicked Melody" frequently accompanies Kuja when he is walking on screen and talking to characters, or otherwise engaging in some kind of direct action. The melody introduces two features that become important fixtures in other iterations of Kuja's theme: an organ introduction, and a background beat that has some syncopated features, and sounds a lot like clapping or stomping. Sustained strings play the chromatic melody of Kuja's theme, and the harmonies are similar to those in "Kuja's theme", but performed as simultaneous chords rather than arpeggios.

8.5.3 "Desert Palace Theme"

"Desert Palace Theme" combines the clapping and stomping percussion from Wicked Melody with the piano from Kuja's theme. The result is a type of polyrhythm: while both maintain the same rhythm throughout, the rhythms always seem to be slightly syncopated or off-beat. This track also includes the use of a character theme, although it is actually functioning as a location theme. We have discussed this before in this chapter (The same melody was used in "Garnet's Theme" as in "Crossing These Hills"). In Kuja's case, this correlation is an effective representation of ego; Kuja's grandiose palace embodies his perception of himself (or his ideal self). Kuja's ego also contributes to his animosity towards Zidane (both were created by Garland, but Zidane is considered an upgrade).[99] The music provides the adventuring party with the consistent reminder that they are on Kuja's territory, and a fight with him is imminent. Containing a restrained melody, jarring rhythms, and a short loop, the qualities of this track are very characteristic of dungeon music, but with the added feature of also containing a character theme.

8.5.4 "The Dark Messenger"

"The Dark Messenger" is the battle music that occurs when the party finally fights Kuja at the end of the game. This music contains many

---

[98] *Final Fantasy IX*, Squaresoft, 2000.
[99] Final Fantasy IX *Ultimania.*

stylistic characteristics of battle music, such as drums, rock rhythms, and rock instruments. The use of the organ in this track both references rock-inspired battle music, and Kuja's main theme group. The organ melody at the beginning is actually a component of "Wicked Melody". Kuja's percussive theme is also present in this battle music, although this too dissolves quickly into a drum kit performing a rock rhythm. Many of the other instruments in this boss battle exist in Kuja's thematic group, including the piano, the organ, and percussive instruments, and all undergo transformations in this track. This is reflective of the character's state: Kuja enters "trance mode" in this battle, which is a special form *Final Fantasy IX* character can enter when they have endured significant emotional or physical damage.

8.5.5 "The Final Battle"

A typical conclusion to RPGs such as *Final Fantasy IX* involves the party defeating the game's primary antagonist, only to reveal that there is actually a bigger, more powerful boss in charge of them. In *Final Fantasy IX*, the party defeats Kuja only to reveal Necron, a mysterious boss who claims to represent death itself, and desires to essentially destroy everything. The Necron battle theme itself is divided into four sections, which are preceded by an extensive intro, during which Necron taunts and heckles the party. During the fourth section, an organ plays the outline of Kuja's theme, but in a major key. This theme is near the background of the orchestrational field, but clearly audible. The embedding of Kuja's theme illustrates the fact that it was Kuja who influenced Necron to destroy. The change of the theme to major key is indicative of Necron being, rather than a dark, mysterious and troubled antagonist, an antagonist that exists to kill for the sake of killing.

8.6 Conclusion: *Final Fantasy IX*

This text has only examined a couple of the thematic groups used in *Final Fantasy IX*; there are many other character themes, location themes, and concept themes throughout that are just as effective at aiding characterization and story development. It is also important to consider how thematic groups are used to expose and illustrate key features of the game. "Terra's Theme" and "Melodies of Life" both reference origin, or the sense of home, although in different ways. "Terra's Theme" represents the concept of home as a feeling, which is what Zidane was made to believe in. The theme group referenced Zidane's origin, and eventually, he discovered this previously unknown origin. The discovery made him question what and who he was, and it was his friends that reminded him that it didn't matter where he came from. While the game displayed Garnet consistently recalling the song from her memory, the game never referenced Zidane attempting to recall anything from his past. "Melodies of Life" and its component themes were also associated with memory and origin, although primarily the origin of Garnet, both as a summoner and a child. Unlike Zidane, Garnet had more of a feeling of not belonging, and questioned her past throughout the game. The discovery of her origin as a summoner led her to find herself, which in turn made her confident. Both Zidane and Garnet had different approaches to how they felt about origin, but in the end they informed one another, and also made the discovery that one's experiences in life and the friends they kept contributed to who they were as a person. This theme of origin is also important in the game for other characters such as Vivi, a manufactured Black Mage, who, although he was originally designed to simply be a soulless doll of destruction for the Queen, was aware and conscious. Vivi's constant searching for his past and origin also remained constant in the game, and it was Vivi narrating at the end who thanked Kuja for assuring them that they were not "created for the wrong reasons", and continued to narrate through each character's concluding scene.[100] Additionally, it is the "Song From Her Memory", which contains Theme B of the Melodies of Life them, that is played during the character conclusions at the end of the game, rather than each character's personal theme.

8.7 Cyclic Themes

Cyclic form includes any type of multi-movement work in which many movements use the same theme in some form.[101] The technique has a complex history, having fallen into disuse in the Baroque and Classical eras, but steadily increasing in use during the nineteenth century.[102] Some of the earlier examples of cyclic form include the Renaissance Cyclic Mass, in which movements of the mass contain music based on the same cantus firmus, or chant melody.[103] This type of thematic use is present in video games as well, and *Halo: Combat Evolved* provides an excellent example, as components of the main theme are present in many tracks of

[100] *Final Fantasy IX*, Squaresoft, 2000.

[101] Macdonald, Hugh. 2001. "Cyclic Form". *The New Grove Dictionary of Music and Musicians*, second edition, edited by Stanley Sadie and John Tyrrell. London: Macmillan Publishers.

[102] Randel, Don Michael. 2003. "Cyclic Form". *The Harvard Dictionary of Music*, fourth edition, Cambridge, MA: Belknap Press.

[103] Burkholder, J. Peter. 2001. "Borrowing, §5: Renaissance Mass Cycles". *The New Grove Dictionary of Music and Musicians*, second edition, edited by Stanley Sadi and John Tyrell. London: Macmillan Publishers.

the soundtrack. Unlike the use of themes in *Final Fantasy IX*, however, the use of thematic content in *Halo* is not used to provide character development or aid in storytelling, but to create a consistent musical backdrop for the setting of the game. The cyclic mass actually provides a good starting point for examining the use of cyclic themes in games, as these masses have very easily identifiable means of modification. We will briefly examine those techniques and how they are implemented in Renaissance music. Later in the chapter, we will see how this corresponds to the settings of the *Halo* theme. Additionally, *Halo* itself has religious undertones, and while it may not have been Martin O'Donnell's intention to create music that uses techniques derived from Renaissance music, there is a stylistic similarity between Gregorian chant and the opening of the *Halo* theme. I describe two of the techniques that Martin O'Donnell uses in *Halo* below:

1) A **Motto mass** (or head motive mass), is a polyphonic mass in which the movements are linked primarily by sharing the same opening motive or phrase.[104] In the Halo theme, there is a rhythmic string/drum motive (which will be discussed later) that is used in a similar fashion throughout Halo, with the entry of the motive being the most recognizable.

2) A **cantus-firmus mass** is a polyphonic mass in which the same cantus firmus (existing melody) is used in each movement.[105] This technique is also used to great effect in the Halo soundtrack; the opening of the main theme contains a Gregorian chant-like melody that is present in many of the other tracks.

Following the Renaissance, cyclic form became less prominent, and Baroque and most Classical multi-movement works frequently made use of completely different themes in each movement. However, the technique saw revival during the Romantic era, and while several composers, including Mendelssohn and Schubert, used cyclic forms at some point, one of the most famous examples remains Hector Berlioz's *Symphonie Fantastique*. The work incorporates a theme, titled an idée fixe, in every single movement. The term was devised by Berlioz and refers to a melody that is used throughout a piece to represent a person, thing, or idea, transforming it to suit the mood and situation.[106] This

---

[104]Burkholder, J. Peter, and Donald Jay Grout. A *History of Western Music: Ninth International Student Edition*. WW Norton & Company, 2014.
[105] Ibid.
[106] Ibid.

sounds very similar to a leitmotif, however, an idée fixe involves a singular theme, that may exist almost to the point of obsession, rather than a collection of different motives that are recognizable. We will discuss later why this application becomes so relevant to AAA recent-gen titles.

8.8 Halo: Combat Evolved, Theme

To have a discussion about the use of themes in *Halo: Combat Evolved*, it is necessary to have an understanding of the components of the Halo theme. The two primary sections of the Halo theme are: 1) a Gregorian chant-like melody, which I will title section A, and 2) a rhythmic strings and drum theme, which I will title section B. The overall form of the Combat evolved theme, therefore, is ABA:

> 0:00-0:33: Section A
> 0:34-2:23: Section B
> 2:34-end: Section A

TRACK NAME	HALO THEME	TRANSFORMATIONS
Brothers in Arms	Section B	Retains string drum rhythm, changed melodic and harmonic elements
Enough Dead Heroes	Section A	Strings/brass play A theme at beginning/end
Perilous Journey	Section B	Electronic sounds play ascending strings motive variation from section B
The Gun Pointed at the Head of the Universe	Section B	Same drums as in section B, and in some areas same drum rhythms
Devils... Monsters...	Section B	Strings contain ascending rhythmic motive variation from section B
Covenant Dance	Section A, B	Choral chant melody from section A, Drums from section B, electronic instrument playing variation of ascending rhythmic string motive (B)
Rock Anthem for Saving the World	Section B	Includes drums from section B, rhythmic strings, guitar plays melodies from section B
Drumrun	Section B	Drums from section B with processing
On a Pale Horse	Section A	Strings play a variation of melody from theme A
Suite Autumn	Section A	Melody from A at end and slowed, blended with the strings
Dust and Echoes	Section A	Melody from A throughout, against string/synth pad background

8.9 Conclusion: *Halo* Thematic Use

As is shown in the table above, *Halo* makes use of many different arrangements of each component of its theme during tracks that occur at various parts of the game. This type of thematic use is considerably different from that in *Final Fantasy IX*, as it is not used to tell a story or depict a character's trajectory. Instead the theme is reworked in various ways to connect components of the game to a common setting or tone. This may largely be due to the genre of the game: First Person Shooter games often do contain a storyline, but it is less complex (and shorter in duration) than the storyline of an RPG, as the main component of an FPS will remain its gameplay. Gameplay is important in RPGs, but the story and narrative has always served a more crucial function than in many other game genres. Additionally, because of the genre, the sound and music function differently. Gameplay in *Halo* is conducive to adaptive music: the world is open, with fewer sharp transitions between areas, the sound effects are prominent, and there are no clear distinctions between areas that contain enemies and those that do not (areas are flexible and enemies can appear after they are eliminated). However, none of these concepts are unique to *Halo*, as they are features shared by many action games and shooter games, as we discussed in the previous chapter. The thematic coherence within the *Halo* soundtrack resulted in a musical backdrop that was successful not only as adaptive music, but also as a musical work.[107]

The reason that this is so important is that adaptive music in general, and especially the type of adaptive music that uses, for example, a technique like horizontal re-sequencing, can easily fall into the trap of being too amorphous or too ambiguous. While the leap in interactivity is ideal, a soundtrack runs the risk of losing its individuality because the music has to be constructed in such a way that it can be re-organized and re-constructed without sounding like pieces were put together incorrectly. *Red Dead Redemption*, for example, allowed for short audio stems to be played using generative algorithmic means, but in order for the sound team to make this possible, every single stem was in the key of A minor. Once again, we are presented with the task of creating a wide variety of interesting music with a limited amount of possibilities (in this case, limited by pitch/key). Martin O'Donnell's approach to Halo represents a moderate approach, blending the through-composed methods used in *Final Fantasy IX* with the very liberally adaptive techniques used in *Red Dead Redemption*. This allows the *Halo* soundtrack to function effectively as adaptive, but also to have very distinct and recognizable themes.

8.10 Thematic Function in Post-HD Games

This section describes the use of themes in post-HD video games, a generation of games that includes more adaptive music, lower volumes of in-game music, and higher quality FMVs. Realism during gameplay is very much emphasized, which may partially be why the soundtrack music starts to play a quieter role - we don't hear continuous background

---

[107] Shephard, Tim, and Anne Leonard. *The Routledge Companion to Music and Visual Culture*. Routledge, 2013, p. 181.

music as we explore our own environment, but we do hear sounds and respond accordingly. However, game themes and cinematic approaches to music in games are increasing. Title sequences are becoming more tightly crafted, and FMVs contain very clear and emotional use of themes. Therefore, music's role in games is not diminishing; rather, it is changing. This section discusses the use of themes as derived from cinematic practices, as well as some of the approaches to themes that can be used in adaptive music. These examples will also illuminate why Martin O'Donnell's approach in *Halo* is so important, and influential on this generation of games.

8.10.1 Cinematic Paradigms

One musical trend that we see in the most recent games, especially post-Dolby Digital, is the use of music in a similar fashion to that of film. Part of this is related to the general style of the music (game music tends to incorporate more orchestra, extensive title sequences and incidental music cues), but it also pertains to the placement of the music within the game. This is likely due to the increased realism in the game, especially regarding the sonic environment. During a film, music tends to be most present during periods of high emotional tension, and decreases in volume and presence when, for example, characters are talking onscreen. Video games now often use similar patterns in their use of music, removing or attenuating musical elements during dialogue and heavy sound effects, and increasing the amount of incidental cues that occur. This may be considered a natural result of the evolution of games, as sound effects become more analogous to real world sound effects or movie sound effects. The cinematic influence also results from the increasing popularity of video game music, video game music symphonies, and the industry of video game music. Like film scores, video game scores may now be composed for large orchestras, with a lot of development put into the music for the game. However, also like film scores, video game scores (at least for AAA titles) are becoming ever more relegated to the background during periods of activity.

8.10.2 Applications in Heavily Adaptive Soundtracks

With the increase in adaptive music, an important consideration becomes the use of thematic material that is recognizable while also retaining the capability for music to be fluid. This is a complicated concern. When examining the themes for *Final Fantasy IX* discussed previously, for example, it is clear that to stop playback of a specific theme and begin playback of another (due to a scene change) would not result in a smooth transition. *Final Fantasy IX* includes screen fades and clearly delineated areas, and the music provides an analogue to this. However, in recent-gen 3D games, this becomes a concern because the areas are open, without fade screens, and the music changes adaptively. This presents problems for the creation of the type of lengthy melodies in *Final Fantasy IX*, which have clear and obvious beginnings and ends. Additionally, techniques such as vertical re-orchestration and horizontal re-sequencing require composers and sound teams to write and produce materials that are capable of being combined in several different ways, both instrumentally and sequentially, without sounding haphazard or clashing. As discussed previously, this type of music does affect how composers approach the actual materials, and it also changes the effect that re-orchestration will have on the emotion of the music. If the music is continuously adapting, the minor changes that Uematsu used to such great effect in *Final Fantasy IX,* for example, will have substantially less gravity because they will occur all the time, and not necessarily with relation to narrative and characterization. This also may be why a cyclic approach is so favourable for soundtracks that are heavily immersive and contain significant degrees of adaptivity.

8.10.3 Destiny *(2014)* and the Halo *Legacy*
Martin O'Donnell and Michael Salvatori's work on the Halo series paved the way for other soundtracks to become more immersive and adaptive, and the cyclic thematic use allowed for the creation of music that was unifying, but also very diverse. Cyclic use of themes does differ from leitmotif approaches, because unlike the use of leitmotif, it does NOT need to be easily recognizable and identifiable, and it is not associated (necessarily) with a specific person, place, or idea. The use of a common theme or themes throughout will give the music a subtle sense of unification that may or may not be obviously apparent to the player. Since we examined one of Martin O'Donnell's pioneering works using this type of composition, the *Halo* soundtrack, earlier in the chapter, this section will conclude with an examination of his final contribution under employment by Bungie, the soundtrack to *Destiny* (2014). *Destiny* is also an FPS like *Halo*, although the gameplay is primarily online. It also involves some RPG elements, which add to the complexity of the gameplay. However, the primary gameplay mechanics are FPS and the environment is fully 3D and very immersive. Therefore, the game does have extreme realism, immersion, and very fast-paced action, just like *Halo*. The soundtrack has a rich background, and involved primarily a collaboration between Martin O' Donnell and Paul McCartney, but several other composers also worked on the soundtrack, including Michael Salvatori and C. Paul Johnson. The soundtrack was recorded with a 102-person orchestra at Abbey Road studios, and along with 44

tracks that were released on the OST, Paul McCartney recorded and produced a track of his own.[108] The theme of *Destiny*, called "The Traveller", is similar in structure to the *Halo* theme, opening with a melodic motive in the horns, and progressing through a more activated section including higher strings, voice, and pizzicato strings, and also through a fast section with low rhythmic strings, similar to the string/drum section in *Halo*. These different elements of the main theme are dispersed throughout the soundtrack, and expanded upon to create entire tracks – this technique was also used in the *Halo* soundtrack, as we have seen earlier. Therefore, the legacy of the sound and music in *Halo* continues to have an impact on current game music.

8.10.3 The Mass/Idée Fixe Connection

At the beginning of this chapter, we discussed both cantus firmus mass and idée fixe, and their use in cyclic forms. However, it may remain questionable why these are appropriate comparisons to draw, considering the use of cyclic form may also be present in film, a media which is far less (at least temporally) removed from video games. However, there are many parallels between these types of music and their place in history, and cyclic form in games, and its place in video game music history. The cantus firmus mass, for example, was used during a time (in the 15th century) when polyphonic textures in choral music had grown incredibly dense. In fact, in the early 16th century, polyphony was reportedly banned from use in the church because the saturation of the lines had made it nearly impossible to discern the actual words of the text (while the reported potential banning may be a rumour, Palestrina was aware of the need for discernible text in sacred music, and such discourse highlights the complexity of polyphonic music at the time).[109] Using a cantus firmus or motif as a basis for every movement, or nearly every movement, may have been an early attempt at unifying something that had become extremely complex. This same concept can be seen in the music of Berlioz and his idée fixe; orchestral music especially had expanded to extremes, including in musical duration and in the size of the orchestra. A typical Mozart symphony from the mid-18th century, for example, would have been approximately 25 minutes in length, with an orchestra of 30-60 players, while Berlioz's *Sypmohonie Fantastique,* composed in 1830, was longer than an hour in duration, and contained

---

[108] McCaffrey, Ryan. "Bungie's Destiny: A Land of Hopes and Dreams." Imagine Games Network online, Feb 17, 2013, http://ca.ign.com/articles/2013/02/17/bungies-destiny-a-land-of-hope-and-dreams, accessed May 6, 2017.

[109] Jerome Roche, *Palestrina* (Oxford Studies of Composers, 7, New York: Oxford University Press, 1971.

closer to 100 players in the orchestra.[110] Once again, the sound had become complex and saturated. Each of these examples, discussed above, represents a heavy saturation point in its period in history. This is very similar to the trajectory taken in video games. The "size" of the orchestra has increased, from the 5-channel NES to the current systems that use full orchestra, a full sound effect palette, and surround sound. Therefore, AAA HD fast action games contain a very large aural load in comparison to, for example, *Final Fantasy IX*. *Final Fantasy IX* contained only written dialogue, minimal sound effects, and clearly delineated areas. Therefore, the player could focus more of their aural attention on the music only, allowing the type of melodically rich music that Uematsu excelled at, as well as the numerous themes (in *Final Fantasy IX*, there are 11 character themes alone). With the high sonic saturation level in games such as *Halo* or *Destiny*, it becomes very difficult to internalize and identify so many differing themes, which is perhaps why using a singular cyclic theme and its internal components can allow for a very unified sound. Therefore, this approach to music may become very important to future soundtracks of this game type, in order to create effective soundtracks that are also memorable.

8.11 Chapter Conclusion

Themes are an incredibly powerful tool in guiding the media consumer towards certain emotions, to recognize certain characters, places, or concepts, and also to allude to things subtextually. Themes have been used successfully in film, opera, TV shows, and other forms of media, but function equally as well in video games. They can also serve multiple functions, such as character development and storytelling, or maintaining a sense of unity within a game. Using a consistent theme throughout can improve the interactive capabilities of the sound as it can make techniques such as vertical re-orchestration and horizontal re-sequencing more feasible and flexible whilst retaining game or concept identity. Thematic use, whether as a leitmotif, which must remain discernible regardless of transformation, or as cyclic form, in which themes may not retain their overt identity, provides unity to game music. In both game examples we have examined above, we can deconstruct tracks and describe the occurrence of the theme as well as how it has been transformed, although the themes are more easily identified with superficial listening in *Final Fantasy IX*. Identifiable themes are becoming less and less prevalent in games, especially with the rise of

---

[110] Burkholder, J. Peter, and Donald Jay Grout. *A History of Western Music: Ninth International Student Edition*.

adaptive music and the increase in sound effect volume. Music often exists in the background of scenes, and requirements are placed on sound teams to make music as interactive and/or as seamlessly adaptive as possible. Additionally, some games are moving towards music that is in some aspect generative music. At the same time, cinematic themes are becoming more prevalent in games. However, these more often occur during cut scenes and title screens or credits, and less often during active gameplay. This can be seen as a reflection of games becoming more realistic and immersive, and also more like cinema (background music does not play continuously). However, even in cinema, where music has always functioned as to be heard in the background, cues and short clips of music usually relate to theme groups, much like *Final Fantasy IX*. And with such a push towards nostalgia gaming and games in recent years, it is becoming apparent that players do appreciate memorable and identifiable themes.

Chapter 9: Conclusion

Following the completion of this text, you should have gained a greater understanding of the study of video game music, and you should have a basic toolkit available to you with which to analyze, write about, comment on, and evaluate the function of game music. You should be able to trace the historical trajectory of game music and explain some of the reasons behind the developments. You should also be aware of the importance of the study of video game music, and why this music is such a prominent fixture in contemporary culture. While this text is not a manual on how to compose for video games, aspiring or working composers in the industry should benefit from the discussions of compositional and theoretical techniques, which can be applied to future compositions.

9.1 Video Game Music History

This text covered the history of video game music, from the late 1970s, when music began to appear consistently in arcade games, through the present (in this case 2016). This is not a significantly lengthy period of time, but in this short period, game music underwent tremendous growth and change. The first game to have continuous background sound was *Space Invaders* (1978), and consisted of a continuously repeating four-note pattern. Today games can contain hours and hours of pre-recorded and streamed audio, most of which can be programmed to change continuously throughout the game. Some concepts, however, have remained throughout history, such as the responsiveness of the music to gameplay. The sounds in *Space Invaders*, for example, sped up as the player got closer to failure and slowed down when the player began to succeed again, and this type of adaptive response is present in current games, when sounds increase in volume, change in instrumentation, or adapt in other ways. Therefore, while there are many differences in the actual sound of game music, some of the core functionality of the music remains the same. It is important to recognize the impact of technology on the development of game music, as these limitations led to the amount, duration, and type of sound that could be played back on any given console or computer device. The NES, for example, contained only five channels of sound, with many limitations on what types of sounds could be produced. Such limitations do not exist today, and composers are free to do what they wish, including substantial post-production of sound material before it is programmed into a game. Such technological limitations have informed the style of music and its development. The evolution of game sound function also played an integral role. In the 1970s and 1980s, music was added to arcade games (mostly during the title screen) to lure customers, as the loudest games attracted the most people. As sound technology became more accessible and game music became longer and more individual, the intended function became more about creating individual and unique soundtracks, rather than flashy and loud sound. This evolved further once 3D gaming and surround sound entered living rooms, with sound and music both serving to immerse the player in a realistic gaming experience. However, while the function has changed considerably over time, all of these uses emerged out of a desire to sell more games, and to keep players actively gaming.

This fast development of video game music, which included rapid changes over a period of about four decades, has seen scholarly reflection only in very recent years. Some publications have been produced regarding the study of game music, and many dissertations (especially since 2012) have begun to discuss elements of game music. Prior to these publications, most books discussing video game music were written for aspiring game composers, and took a more commercial approach. Therefore, the reflection on video game music and its development as a scholarly subject is actually quite new. This reflectiveness can also be seen outside scholarship, with the rise in nostalgia gaming, including the re-release of old games and the development of new games that are modeled after past generations of games. One thing that has remained clear is the importance of music and sound in games, which will continue to have an impact on game music and its development. The future of game music is uncertain (as most technologies are), but it is likely that we will see evolution in immersive sound, with the advent of virtual reality technologies, as well as increases in music composed for nostalgia gaming. The market share of applications and downloadable games also has an impact on game music, as these games have different musical demands. The primary discoveries following the historical study in this text are:

1) Video game music is informed by technology,
2) The overall function of video game music is continuously changing, but consistently aims to attract players,
3) Reflection upon video game music will have an impact on its future development, and
4) The future of video game music is uncertain, but will likely result in several differing trajectories.

9.2 Theoretical Concepts

In this second unit of this text we examined the theoretical concepts of video game music, including terminology related to music for interactive media, the function of music within a game, and the ways in which game music uses themes for storytelling, characterization, and musical cohesiveness. Because this text is intended to be an introduction for anyone, including those that do not have a strong background in music, more detailed formal analyses and those involving specific harmonic or pitch analysis were left out. However, you should have an understanding upon completion of this text on concepts related to video game music, such as the differing degrees of interactivity (reactive, adaptive, and fully interactive), the way in which music is made to be indefinite (looping, dynamic looping, and generative music), and whether the music can be heard by the in-game characters (diegetic vs. non-diegetic). Once again, these are concepts that, while they have been written about to a degree, have not reached the academic mainstream, and certainly no unified scholarly definitions exist. However, it is crucial not to lump all game music into a singular category, such as interactive, or looping, without understanding how it functions with regards to gameplay, and what techniques are used to create music that is both engaging and indefinite. Currently the term interactive is difficult to define even within academic electronic music, despite being consistently written about, and many texts and articles about video games term the music interactive, taking for granted the meaning of the term with respect specifically to the music (interactive media does not automatically indicate the music is interactive). The fact that video games are a media with indefinite time is also pertinent to the study of the music; this implies a radical difference in both the compositional process (unlike film composers, video game composers do not have the ability to play the game from start to finish and set the music to picture lock) as well as the approach to the sound. Composers cannot even determine an approximate amount of time a player will remain in any given area of the game, as this can vary substantially from player to player. Therefore, several approaches to indefinite music have emerged, beginning with the concept of linear looping (repeating the same piece of music over and over), developing into more dynamic forms of looping, which include modifications of a continuously looped piece of music, and eventually giving way to other alternatives such as generative music, which is a type of music created in real time based on some kind of pre-written algorithm. All of these types of indefinite music have compositional merit, and their use is very much determined by the type of gameplay and game that they occur in.

You should also be aware of the form and function of game music, and the way in which music relates to gameplay. Music differs depending on the area of the game it occurs in; many of the stylistic traits of music in these situations have developed out of gameplay paradigms that were present in the very beginning of video game history. Music functions as a result of what is going on in the game; therefore, during a battle the music will be considerably different than when the player is in a safe area of the game. This concept applies to game genre as well, as genre is determined by gameplay mechanics. Between the mechanics of gameplay, possible audience, game setting, and even psychological factors, the genre of a game will have an influence on the style and type of music used within. Finally, use of themes in video games remains an important component to the compositional organization; many RPGs make use of extensive libraries of themes for individual characters, events, or places, using such themes as leitmotifs. Other games, including more immersive and fast-paced games like *Halo*, use the continuous use and reworking of a small group of themes in a way that creates a unifying sound, a concept related to cyclic form. Just as with many of the other theoretical concepts, the integration of themes in games is highly depended on gameplay and function of music within the game. The primary discoveries related to theoretical constructs in games discussed in this book are:

1) An appropriate analysis of game music will consider how it functions as a music for interactive media,
2) Function and placement of music is an important determinant of its features, and
3) Themes can be used effectively in numerous ways in video games.

9.3 Onwards

Following the completion of this text, the reader should have a very clear understanding of these basic concepts relating to video game music, including:

1) An understanding of the basic history of game music,
2) A framework for analysing game music theoretically,
3) An understanding of the social and cultural impact of video game music.

For further understanding of game music, you can examine the references cited within this text, and find your own sources on the subject, as the body of literature on video game music continues to grow. Game music is continuously in evolution, and as more analysis and evaluation is made on music in games, these analyses may affect future game music. Therefore, this text should not be seen as a definitive solution to all analysis of game music, but as a good basic framework from which one can begin their examination of the genre.

Selected Bibliography

Burkholder, J. Peter. "Borrowing, §5: Renaissance Mass Cycles". *The New Grove Dictionary of Music and Musicians*, second edition, edited by Stanley Sadi and John Tyrell. London: Macmillan Publishers, 2001.

Collins, Karen. *Game sound: an introduction to the history, theory, and practice of video game music and sound design*. Mit Press, 2008.

Collins, Karen. *Playing with sound: a theory of interacting with sound and music in video games*. Mit Press, 2013.

Drummond, Jon. "Understanding interactive systems." *Organised Sound* 14.02 (2009): 124-133.

Horowitz, Steve, and Scott R. Looney. *The Essential Guide to Game Audio: The Theory and Practice of Sound for Games*. CRC Press, 2014.

Hughes, William, and Maryanne Cline Horowitz, ed. "Genre," *New Dictionary of the History of Ideas 3* (2005): 912-918.

Johnson, David. "Round". *The New Grove Dictionary of Music and Musicians*, second edition, edited by Stanley Sadie and John Tyrell. London: Macmillan Publishers, 2001.

Macdonald, Hugh. "Cyclic Form". *The New Grove Dictionary of Music and Musicians*, second edition, edited by Stanley Sadie and John Tyrrell. London: Macmillan Publishers, 2001.

Medina-Gray, Elizabeth. *Modular Structure and Function in Early 21st-Century Video Game Music*. Yale University, 2014.

Newcomb, David Lawrence. *The Fundamentals of the Video Game Music Genre*. James Madison University, 2012.

Phillips, Winifred. *A composer's guide to game music*. MIT Press, 2014.

Randel, Don Michael. "Cyclic Form". *The Harvard Dictionary of Music*, fourth edition, Cambridge, MA: Belknap Press, 2003.

Roche, Jerome. *Palestrina*. Oxford Studies of Composers, Vol. 7. New York: Oxford University Press, 1971.

Rowe, Robert. *Interactive music systems: machine listening and composing*. MIT press, 1992.

Shephard, Tim, and Anne Leonard. *The Routledge companion to music and visual culture*. Routledge, 2013.

Sweet, Michael. *Writing Interactive Music for Video Games: A Composer's Guide*. Pearson Education, 2014.

Wegele, Peter. *Max Steiner: Composing, Casablanca, and the Golden Age of Film Music*. Rowman & Littlefield, 2014.